The
HUNGER
STRIKES

The
HUNGER
STRIKES

R. K. Walker

LAGAN
BOOKS

© 2006 Lagan Books, Belfast
All Rights Reserved

First Published 2006
by Lagan Books
ISBN 1904684181

A CIP record for this book is available from the British Library

Typeset in Garamond
Printed and bound in the EU

Photos © Pacemaker Press,
except 5. © Mal McCann
Used with permission

Author's Note

This book's existence owes a considerable debt to those who gave interviews to the author. On the Republican side, I'm grateful to Séanna Walsh, Laurence McKeown, Bik McFarlane, Tommy McKearney, Johnny Donaghy, Billy Leonard and other Republicans. Thanks also to Richard McAuley for permission to reproduce one of the prisoners' comms to the Relatives Action Committee. I am grateful, too, for the contributions from former prison staff of various ranks as well as former RUC, UDR and British Army personnel, who wish to remain nameless.

Considerable research was carried out on the Loyalist side by the journalist and author of the best-selling *The Billy Boy: the life and death of Billy Wright,* Chris Anderson, for which I'm much obliged. I am also indebted to Chris for access to contributions from former government ministers, former intelligence operatives and southern contacts. Thanks, too, to Sean Farren, former chairman of the SDLP, for taking time out of a busy Stormont schedule in July 2004 to meet the author. Thanks also to journalist Colm Heatley and Bernadette McAliskey. Thanks to Ciarán O'Pronntaigh, former editor of Irish language daily newspaper, *Lá.*

Words of thanks are also due to Irish author Tim Pat Coogan, not only for his time but also for access to his vast knowledge of the history and overall context of the subject, which has been a source of inspiration as well as information. I am also grateful for the patience of the publishers of this book, and the faith they have shown in sticking with this project, despite many false finishes.

Thanks also to my editor, Allan Burnett, whose expertise moulded the raw text into a book. Thanks, also, to all my family.

Finally, any book on the hunger strikes of 1980-1 has to recognise the contribution made to Irish history by, and the sacrifices of, the hunger strikers themselves, their families and their comrades. Many on all sides of the conflict suffered grief. Grief is not a bigot – it can visit anyone. Many families made sacrifices over those 35 years with, as one contributor points out, "no murals to remember them by". At the time of writing, in November 2005, that would all appear to be behind us. For many reasons, I personally believe that is in no small way due to the conscious sacrifice of the hunger strikers, among many, many others, from all communities involved in the conflict.

Contents

List of Pictures

1. H-block "dirty protest"
2. Bobby Sands's funeral
3. Rioting at Divis flats
4. Hunger-strike demonstration
5. Long Kesh prison hospital cell
6. Gerry Adams
7. Funeral of Joe McDonnell
8. Annual hunger-strike march

All except 5. © Pacemaker Press
5. © Mal McCann

Front Cover
H-block "dirty protest"

Back Cover.
The Hunger Strikers
© Pacemaker Press

Introduction

The hunger strikes that began in the H-blocks of the Maze/Long Kesh prison on March 1, 1981, have been credited by some with starting the peace process in Northern Ireland. For others, they elongated "The Long War". Whether or not the peace process can be traced directly to the hunger strikes is something for debate, yet the very least the strikes achieved was the politicisation of a generation of Nationalists and the radicalisation of a generation of Republicans. The hunger strikes invigorated and, some would say, effectively created Provisional Sinn Fein as a political force for change – and Sinn Fein became a vehicle for the peace process.

When the hunger strikes were called off, in October 1981, few beyond the most committed Republicans could have envisaged the outcome as any sort of victory. On the contrary, it seemed Republicanism had been dealt a crushing blow. Yet many in the IRA leadership guessed that, behind the façade of apparent defeat, the hunger strikes had secured an auspicious development: the shifting of the mainstream Nationalist consensus onto a more radical agenda. Some Republicans guessed that, far from finishing the IRA, the outcome of 1981 would be a propaganda harvest unsurpassed since Sinn Fein's historic 1918 election victory – or perhaps even since the Easter Rising of 1916. Of course, they recognised as much as anyone that whatever had been achieved, had been so at a fearsome price. Indeed, the leadership had been at pains to avoid the hunger strike that the prisoners were determined to go on.

Today, Provisional Sinn Fein is the largest Nationalist political party in the "Six Counties" (as Northern Ireland is known to Nationalists), having overtaken the SDLP. Sinn Fein has had two members sitting in the Northern Ireland Executive, holding the Health and Education portfolios prior to the suspension of the Northern Ireland Assembly in 2002. In addition, the Westminster parliamentary seat won by IRA hunger striker Bobby

Sands in 1981 is once again in Republican hands, as are four others. Indeed, the legitimacy of Republican ideals is now accepted among northern Nationalists to the degree that Mark Durkan, leader of the SDLP, considered it advantageous to contend during the 2005 general election campaign that the SDLP was a "Republican" party.

South of the border, too, the influence of Sinn Fein is growing. The party has five members in the Dail – and although Fianna Fail has ostentatiously ruled out considering Sinn Fein as a coalition partner in a future government, the fact that such a possibility became an issue at all is testament to Provisional Sinn Fein's political muscle. Without question, the political landscape of Northern Ireland, and its perspective in relation to both London and Dublin, has changed beyond recognition since 1981. And while many subsequent factors have contributed to this, few, if any, have been more important than the hunger strikes.

This book offers an insight into how the hunger strikes changed the face of northern Irish politics through the voices of those who lived the events. The contributors gathered here articulate the powerful psychological impression that is made when people consciously starve themselves to death for an ideal, and for a larger struggle that they know is unlikely to be resolved until long after they are dead. The wide range of perspectives gathered together in these pages demonstrates the extent to which the hunger strikes convinced Republicans, Nationalists and even their opponents that the *moral* authority of British rule in the north of Ireland could be challenged.

The question of how deeply the hunger strikes undermined the perceived jurisdiction of the state of Northern Ireland (among Nationalists at least) is fundamental to assessing their impact on the subsequent peace process. It can only be answered by recourse, first, to the historical processes that gave birth to the hunger-strike movement and consideration of the pedigree of this type of protest in Anglo-Irish politics. The hunger strikes in the H-blocks were conceived primarily as resistance against a policy known as "criminalisation", the implementation of which had been determinedly pursued by successive British governments for a number of years. Criminalisation was an attempt to treat Republican (and Loyalist) prisoners as common criminals involved in criminal acts, as opposed to political prisoners fighting against what they saw as an unjust state.

Some would say that while criminalisation was ostensibly pitted against both Republican and Loyalist prisoners, the fact that British forces were later demonstrated in official reports (Cory and Stevens) to have colluded with Loyalist paramilitaries undermines the notion that the measure was designed to be used against both sides equally. After all, so continues this view, it was only Republicans who wanted to "overthrow the state", while Loyalists claimed to be protecting it.

To understand the mindset of those who resisted being branded common criminals, to the point where they were prepared to fast to the death, it is necessary to examine why the British government was compelled to try to reinforce Northern Ireland's jurisdiction through criminalisation. The circumstances surrounding that state's birth, Nationalists would contend, ensured such a state would grow up entangled in conflict and shrouded in grey legal status. This perceived dubiety of the state's legal and moral status created an environment where the expression "one man's terrorist is another man's freedom fighter" could find no better home.

The threat to the state of Northern Ireland is not the only vital issue to be considered when assessing the impact of the hunger strikes. There is also the degree to which they challenged the position of militant Republicans. Did the electoral successes of Bobby Sands, Kieran Doherty and Paddy Agnew (the latter two elected to Dail Eireann) during the tumultuous spring and summer of 1981 illustrate a political alternative to armed struggle to those previously reluctant to consider such an option? Did the hunger strikes, moreover, lay the foundations of Sinn Fein's political achievements? And if so, could 1981 actually be considered the most significant Republican victory since 1916? According to historian and author Tim Pat Coogan, a leading authority on the IRA and who contributes valuable insights into the issues raised here, "the hunger strikes *were* the northerner's 1916".

In building on the work of others who have examined the hunger strikes and their place in the history of Ireland, due acknowledgement must be given most notably to the excellent, blow-by-blow account of David Beresford's *Ten Men Dead* and the essential *Nor Meekly Serve My Time* edited by Brian Campbell, Laurence McKeown and Felim O'Hagan.

This book intends to let those who were involved or otherwise affected by the hunger strikes tell it as they saw it. The hunger strikes were a reaction to history; a reaction that went on to cause its own history. Consequently, many other events in the course of the Troubles are related by the author and contributors. Some pertain directly to the hunger strikes, others to associated issues and circumstances. The cruelty that turned teenagers into "terrorists" or "freedom fighters", depending on your view, the collusion that built a laboratory of "dirty war" and the compassion that made peace a possibility are some of the issues brought into sharp relief by the hunger strikes. I hope that by retaining my subjects' organic recollections of earlier and later events during their consideration of the core period, this book serves to further illustrate the meteoric impact that the hunger strikes of 1981 had on the collective consciousness of the people of the Six Counties/ Northern Ireland.

Some contributors' names have been changed to protect their identities.

Chapter One:

A state born in protest

The victory of Bobby Sands, an IRA hunger striker, in the by-election for the Westminster parliamentary seat of Fermanagh-South Tyrone in April 1981, had a profound impact on the thinking of many in the Irish Republican Movement. At that time they had been waging a paramilitary campaign for more than a decade against what they saw as injustice and discrimination against Northern Ireland's Catholic minority and, ultimately, for the reunification of Ireland as a republic of thirty-two counties. Sands's victory ignited a debate that had been smouldering for some time as to the role that could be played by constitutional politics in what remained, at its core, an armed struggle. It opened up, for many, the possibility of a non-violent future for the movement – a future in which Sinn Fein could become a major political force. Nevertheless, it is vital to remember that contrary to being conceived of as a denunciation of military means, the original intention behind the 1980-1 hunger strikes and their related political activities was to express the legitimacy of armed struggle itself. The ten men who died had gone on hunger strike to demand recognition not as politicians, but as prisoners of war.

In order to understand why those motivated to join the IRA or INLA were so convinced of the rightness of their cause and of the legitimacy of armed struggle, to the degree that they were prepared to die for the objective of POW status, it is necessary to take note of some key facts surrounding the creation of the state of Northern Ireland, and how they looked to Nationalists.

The conviction among Republican prisoners that they were POWs held by an occupying foreign government was rooted in the controversial circumstances surrounding the partition of Ireland and creation of the state of Northern Ireland in 1921. It was these circumstances that alienated generations of Nationalists and Republicans from the northern Irish state, and by extension from that state's system of law and order. "Law and order" in Northern Ireland was, in the eyes of many Nationalists, the law and order of the "victor over the oppressed", rather than that of a community of equals working from consensually agreed principles of justice. The notion of what was and what was not a "criminal act" became immediately contentious. Moreover, since Nationalists considered Britain's role to be the guarantor of such an "illegal state-let", British lectures on the morality or legality of resistance were invalidated in Nationalist minds. This point was sharpened when British troops came back to Ireland in 1969 and, after initially being presented as "neutral peace keepers", thereafter attempted to enforce what many Nationalists considered the bogus "law and order" of the Unionist Stormont regime.

Even those northern Nationalists who did not advocate physical force refused for more than thirty years to sit in the Northern Ireland parliament. They felt that to become the official opposition to the "inbuilt" Ulster Unionist parliamentary majority and government would be to show a consent to be governed – a consent they had no intention of giving. To do so would be to validate what they regarded as the unjust, oppressive and illegal partition of Ireland by the Unionists and the British in 1921.

Northern Ireland had been created by partitioning the six most north-easterly counties of the nine-county Irish province of Ulster. This move was intended as a compromise solution to the "Irish question", which had gradually come to dominate British politics in the late nineteenth and early twentieth centuries. A clear majority on the island of Ireland aspired to "Home Rule" – self-government within the British Empire, although there was an element already demanding full independence. Three successive Home Rule bills were, however, frustrated – the first by splits in the Liberal government that proposed it in 1886, the second by rejection from the un-elected House of Lords in 1893 and the third, in 1914, by a combination of the threat of paramilitary rebellion by the Ulster Unionists of northeast Ulster (illegally armed by Britain's soon to be enemy, Germany) and the outbreak of the First World War.

The minority of the Irish population that opposed Home Rule during this period, the Unionists, constituted around a quarter of the total. Unionists feared Home Rule would undermine their social and economic position and destroy their Protestant (and British) sense of identity. They were concentrated geographically in the four most north-easterly of Ulster's nine counties – Antrim, Down, Derry/Londonderry and North Armagh.

There were also significant Unionist populations in another two counties, Tyrone and Fermanagh.

The remaining three counties of Ulster – Donegal, Monaghan and Cavan – all had clear majorities of Home Rulers; that is, those who wished for the restoration of the Irish parliament abolished by Britain's incorporating Act of Union in 1800. In their desire for Home Rule, the majorities of these last three counties of Ulster were at one with the rest of Ireland – which comprised of twenty-three counties in the provinces of Connaught, Munster and Leinster. Throughout Ireland, the vast majority of Home Rulers were Roman Catholic by religion – although there were several Protestant Irish Home Rulers, too – while the minority British Unionists were Protestants of varying denominations.

The Irish Home Rulers were represented at Westminster by the Irish Parliamentary Party, led from 1900 by John Redmond. Home Rule, not full independence, was the aim of most of its members. The Irish Parliamentary Party felt it had won the right of the Irish people to self-government through patient, moderate, constitutional campaigning over decades, which had generally convinced most of the electorate in both Britain and Ireland of the justice of the cause – although it must be said that the British electorate often tired of the issue and, indeed, periodically found sympathy for the Ulster Unionists. Nevertheless, had it been left up to the electorate, Home Rule could have been delivered in 1893. As stated, the bill was thwarted by the un-elected House of Lords, despite being passed by a majority in the elected Commons. Although Home Rule dropped off the agenda after the Tories replaced the Liberals in 1895, when the Liberal Party under Henry Campbell-Bannerman was returned with a convincing majority in 1906, the Irish Parliamentary Party members once more had their expectations raised.

The House of Lords still presented an obstacle, but when it rejected the 1909 "People's Budget", which had passed through the elected House of Commons, the Liberal government – now under Herbert Asquith – called an election for the following year to allow the people to vote for or against the budget. The election was won by the Liberals but at the cost of a reduced majority. This meant they now depended on Redmond's Irish Parliamentary Party to deliver on their election promises.

In order to prevent the House of Lords frustrating further Liberal legislation, certain to include another Irish Home Rule bill, Asquith's government presented the Parliament Bill. It sought to terminate the right of the

House of Lords to reject legislation that had successfully gone through the Commons for more than three continuous sessions. Again, the Lords rejected this Liberal legislation and, again, Asquith called a General Election – this time explicitly on the issue of which House of Parliament had constitutional superiority. The Liberals and the Conservatives won the same number of seats at this, the second General Election of 1910. The Liberals were now more than ever dependent on Redmond's Irish Parliamentary Party, which had 84 MPs (including Independent Nationalists). With the votes of Redmond's Party assured, the Parliament Bill was passed. While this eliminated the Lords' parliamentary veto, it also meant Home Rule for Ireland was now inevitable – assuming the government proposed it.

Unionists were alarmed by this new situation. That sense of alarm appeared to be validated in 1912, when the Liberal government introduced the much-anticipated third Home Rule Bill. The Lords could hold it up, certainly, but within two years it would be law. The worst fear of Unionists was about to be realised. Amid a non-violent campaign of mass protest, they continued with already well-developed plans for a Provisional Government of Ulster, to be implemented should Home Rule be granted to Ireland, which by now looked certain.

Just as well-developed were the Ulster Unionists' plans for armed resistance to the government's strategy. Late in 1910, 18 months before the third Home Rule Bill was introduced to the House of Commons, a clandestine committee was formed by the Ulster Unionist Council with the aim of procuring weapons from any source willing to sell them. The committee's task was to form an army that would defend any Ulster Provisional Government. Sir Edward Carson, who became leader of the Ulster Unionists in 1911, despite being himself a Southern Unionist, threatened the authorities with armed resistance. Privately, Carson, also a prominent lawyer, had doubts about such unlawful activity. Yet his resolute public demeanour convinced at least some in the Liberal government that if all his threats were "bluff", as Redmond claimed in discussions with Asquith, they were convincing bluff. No such bluff was necessary on the part of Carson's northern Unionist partner in opposition to Home Rule, Captain James Craig. He was a gifted military organiser with no such doubts about staging an illegal rebellion for this particular cause. Craig had honed his soldering skills in the Boer war of 1899-1902 and was committed to opposing Home Rule, or at least ensuring Ulster would be exempt, if necessary by physical force.

In November 1912, Asquith reiterated his determination to see Home

Rule delivered by stating he would force the bill through parliament if necessary. Unionists came to realise that they lacked the strength and support to derail the apparent inevitability of Irish Home Rule, so instead made the partition of Ulster from any future devolved Ireland their main objective. To this end, in 1913, Carson and Craig's 150,000-strong Unionist militia officially became known as the Ulster Volunteer Force (UVF). The following year, the UVF was armed with, among other items, three million rounds of ammunition purchased from Britain's soon to be enemy, Germany. The haul was landed at Larne and rapidly distributed throughout Ulster by a fleet of vehicles, an apparent logistical miracle given that such activity – wide-scale preparation to mount an illegal armed rebellion – ought to, thought Nationalists, have aroused the suspicion of the authorities. (The Larne gunrunning incident is still celebrated by many Unionists today, including many politicians who insisted on Provisional IRA decommissioning). Claims of double standards appeared, to some, validated by the fact that only three months after the Larne haul, militant Irish Nationalists responded to Carson and Craig's dramatic escalation of the crisis by unloading their own major cache of arms, including 1500 guns, at Howth, Co. Dublin – and were then attacked by the British Army, who killed three people and injured scores more.

This apparent double standard (to Nationalists at least) makes such key episodes pertinent even today among Irish Republicans when considering the legitimacy of political violence against the British state. So when considering the hunger strikes and the motivations of those who participated in them, we should also consider the raison d'etre of the Republican Movement to which they belonged; namely, to undo the partition of Ireland which, in the Nationalist analysis, was brought about by the threat of illegal violence. And, brought about by a conservative British/Unionist establishment – a network of military commanders, civil servants, Tory peers and the King – that permitted the UVF to become weaponised while leaning on Asquith's Liberal government to concede partition against the wishes of the majority of the electorate. The UVF's influential supporters in Britain argued that "Ulster will fight and Ulster will be right", and in March 1914 Asquith appeared to bend under pressure by suggesting that Ulster be excluded from any Home Rule.

The apparent collusion of an armed Unionist militia with conservative forces in the British establishment to subvert Home Rule and bring about partition by a threat of "armed struggle" has provided proof in the minds of of generations of Nationalists and Republicans that genuine principles of democracy and justice were written out of the story of Northern Ireland from the very beginning. Moreover, the UVF's threat of rebellion was seen to have achieved its political aim.

Republicans and some Nationalists today consider such events to have played a formative role in legitimising the concept of armed struggle. In response to the formation and activities of the UVF, Irish Nationalists formed the Irish Volunteers, with numbers reaching 170,000 men, and by July 1914 both the UVF and the Irish Volunteers were openly drilling in preparation for what seemed an inevitable civil war. As far as the British government was concerned, the loyalty of the British Army in Ireland at the time was questionable, due to a number of incidents, most notably the Curragh Mutiny of March 1914, when some senior British Army officers proclaimed that they would not fight against the UVF.

When the war came it was in Europe, not Ireland. Although the Home Rule Bill had passed through the House of Commons, implementation was suspended until such time as the war ended. Irishmen – Protestant and Catholic, Unionist and Nationalist – joined the British Army. Carson's UVF pledged to fully support the war effort. Redmond, now leader of the Irish Volunteers, wanted his men to fight in France for Britain. When this suggestion proved highly unpopular, it was modified to an instruction to "defend Ireland's shores" under the new name of the National Volunteers. While most of the movement accepted this with varying degrees of reluctance, a sizeable grouping of approximately eleven thousand men under Eoin Mac Neil rejected this notion and kept the name Irish Volunteers.

By 1916, it had become apparent that the war, having dragged on for eighteen months, would not end soon. Some Nationalists, suspicious of the British government's resolve in implementing Home Rule in the face of Unionist and conservative British opposition, sought to resolve matters for themselves. On April 24, 1916, Padraig Pearse of the Irish Republican Brotherhood, along with James Connolly, an Edinburgh-born socialist and founder of the Irish Citizens Army, with others, launched what became known as the "Easter Rising". The rebels took over the General Post Office in O'Connell Street, Dublin, where they read out the Proclamation of the Provisional Government of the Irish Republic – which unilaterally announced Ireland's complete independence from Britain.

The rising was put down within the week by British forces, yet it proved to be a turning point in Irish history. Although initially sceptical of the uprising, Irish public opinion gradually turned against Britain as fifteen of the rebels who had surrendered at the GPO were executed by firing squad. The perceived over-reaction by the British radicalised Irish opinion – just as the hunger strikes were to do sixty-five years later.

This sympathy translated into support for the radical Nationalist party, Sinn Fein, founded in November 1905 by Arthur Griffith, which now supported an independent Irish Republic as opposed to Home Rule under the British Crown. The revulsion at Britain's treatment of the prisoners taken during the Easter Rising combined with increasing opposition to the First World War (the proposed implementation of conscription in particular) to drive the Irish electorate into the Republican camp. Perhaps even more crucially, a vast reservoir of hitherto un-enfranchised Irish men and women were given a vote for the very first time by the 1918 Reform Act. At the Westminster general election of that year, Home Rule, so grudgingly offered by Britain – in Irish eyes, at least – was considered no longer enough for the great majority of Ireland's newly expanded electorate. Sinn Fein were the beneficiaries, winning nearly eighty per cent of votes cast. They could not attract the vote of Unionists in Ulster, however, who clearly voted to remain part of the UK.

When Sinn Fein unilaterally set up Dail Eireann (the Irish Parliament) in January 1919, as they felt entitled to do having resoundingly won a mandate via the Westminster general election, the Ulster Unionists and the British viewed it as an illegal gathering. The Unionist would have no truck with the Dail and continued to send their elected representatives to Westminster. Sinn Fein argued that the overwhelming majority of the Irish electorate had voted for it knowing that the party would not send its elected representatives to what it saw as a foreign parliament in London. Dail Eireann's writ now ran in the majority of Ireland's thirty-two counties – the twenty-six that would later become the Irish Free State in 1922, as well as in many Nationalist areas of what would in 1921 be partitioned as "Northern Ireland". It is important to recount these events here, as modern Republicanism in all its forms traces linage back to Dail Eireann, the first elected government of the thirty-two county Irish Republic.

Until the advent of universal male suffrage and Sinn Fein's dramatic victory in 1918, Ireland's political elite was dominated by Anglican Protestants. This elite had a history of persecution and discrimination against Catholics (and, for a time, Presbyterians too) while giving Protestants political, social, religious and economic advantages. Not all Protestants benefited from this

Ascendancy and some, in fact, were among the poorest citizens of Ireland. However, the Ascendancy did mean that all power was in the hands of Protestants.

This was the situation that was about to change forever in the 26 county area of Ireland, which had given Sinn Fein its mandate in 1918. The Unionist of Ulster now feared a reversal of what they considered an advantageous position, in that they would be outnumbered by more than three to one by Irish Nationalists and therefore dominated by a religious, political and national culture that was anathema to them. Northern Unionists were further appalled by the willingness of their Unionist colleagues in the twenty-Six Counties to attempt to negotiate a better deal under Home Rule for the whole island of Ireland – a notion given serious consideration by Carson himself at various times – as opposed to fighting for the partition of Ulster. Ulster Unionists therefore felt that their sense of British, Protestant national identity was under threat and that they would be forced into a subservient role in a Catholic-dominated Irish State.

The British Liberal government, now under David Lloyd George, proceeded – having declared Dail Eireann illegal in September 1919 – with plans to partition Ireland. The six most north-easterly counties of Ireland, Antrim (eighty per cent Protestant, twenty per cent Catholic), Londonderry (fifty-nine per cent Protestant, forty-one per cent Catholic), Down (sixty-nine per cent Protestant, thirty-one per cent Catholic), Armagh (fifty-five per cent Protestant, forty-five per cent Catholic), Tyrone (forty-four per cent Protestant, fifty-six per cent Catholic), and Fermanagh (forty-four per cent Protestant, fifty-six per cent Catholic), would be split from the rest of Ireland, which was an acknowledgement of Unionism being distinct and separate from Nationalism. The Government of Ireland Act 1920 overrode all previous Home Rule bills to became law on December 23rd of that year and Northern Ireland was born to the delight of the Ulster Unionists and the horror of northern Nationalists – who found themselves not only further away from an Irish Republic but also trapped in a new country where their enemy had an inbuilt majority. To northern Nationalists, the irony of one's own land suddenly and unjustly being in "enemy territory" was bitter indeed. Unionists may have noted that had it not been for partition, then that would have been precisely the fate awaiting them.

The Government Of Ireland Act did provide for a Southern parliament but not Dail Eireann, which purported to be the parliament of an independent thirty-two county Irish Republic rather than a twenty-six county

Home Rule parliament. The latter was never established due to what the present south of Ireland government calls the "War of Independence" of 1919-1921 and the subsequent setting up of the twenty-six county Irish Free State in 1921.

Northern Nationalists felt abandoned by the Irish Free State and trapped in the nightmare scenario of a state controlled by their historic foes. Before the First World War there had been two competing forces in Ulster, one Nationalist and one Unionist, each with supposedly equal status under the law. Now the Unionists became, after threatening armed insurrection with the UVF, the force of law and order itself – while the organisation formed in response to the UVF, the Irish Volunteers, (subsequently the IRA) became "terrorists" almost on the flip of a coin.

It could just have easily gone the other way had Britain ever considered it advantageous to let it do so. Indeed, twenty or so years later, British Prime Minister Winston Churchill suggested to the then president of the twenty-six county south, Eamonn De Valera, that he would offer him the other six counties in the northeast if De Valera joined the allies against Hitler. The notion that Britain might have found herself in circumstances where it was expedient to side with Irish Nationalism was not entirely improbable. This flippancy itself further undermined the moral legitimacy of the state of Northern Ireland in the eyes of Irish Nationalists.

Against this background, any attempt to criminalize Republicans who rejected the authority of the Northern Irish state was always going to be resisted. The "law and order" of Northern Ireland was the law and order of victors imposed the political losers, far as Republicans were concerned. To make matters worse, this arrangement was policed and enforced by Nationalists' most ancient enemies. To many Republicans, this went against the laws of natural justice. The legitimate constitutional basis of Irish Nationalism encompassing the whole of Ireland – the democratic mandate for Home Rule in 1912-14 and the election victory of December 1918 – had been, it seemed to Nationalists, usurped by the threat of force by militant Ulster Unionists and their British allies. Not only was this a lesson to Republicans that such methods worked, but crucially it also provided a premise for the moral legitimacy of armed resistance.

Despite attempts to find a compromise that suited everyone, or at least one that caused the least harm, the creation of Northern Ireland failed to stop Nationalists in what they termed the "Six Counties" area of Ireland becoming losers in the deal. Indeed, Nationalists would contend that in "the

North" (as Northern Ireland also became known to them) they were even worse off than before.

In the 1920s, the Nationalist Party took its seats in the Northern Irish Parliament. Many Nationalists had faith that the Boundary Commission, established by the same treaty that established partition, would confirm the borders of the new state in such a way as to ensure those counties containing Catholic majorities joined the Free State, thereby making the convoluted constitutional creation of Northern Ireland an impractical entity. This, it was hoped, would lead everyone – Unionist, British and Irish – to conclude that the border was unworkable and the reunification of Ireland would inevitably follow. However, in 1925, the Boundary Commission confirmed that the Six Counties making up Northern Ireland would remain part of that state.

Other recommendations in the Government of Ireland Act relating to the border and considered favourable to Nationalists were not acted upon as Nationalists had expected. Another safeguard included in the treaty and the setting up of Northern Ireland designed to placate Nationalists trapped within its borders was the use of proportional representation in local elections. When this, too, was discarded in 1929, Nationalists simply lost whatever small amount of faith that they might have had in a system that seemed to be gearing up to exclude them. The Nationalist Party left parliament in protest.

To many Nationalists, these unilateral amendments to various agreements were, if not illegal, certainly immoral. This is an important fact when one bears in mind the legal and moral considerations in taking up arms. In such minds, if democratic procedures had already been stood on their heads in order to suit a particular consistency, then what was wrong with the opposing constituency refusing to accord such a "democracy" sacred status? This Nationalist perception of affairs sustained the rump of the northern IRA and ensured that even those who did not endorse its every belief or action would nonetheless retain varying degrees of sympathy, or at least empathy, for it.

Northern Ireland was thus perceived by Nationalists as a product of Unionist agitation that was in many respects undemocratic and illegal. It was regarded as the ultimate prize by Unionists, to be protected at all costs, but it left many Nationalists feeling plundered. Statements such as "a Protestant country for a Protestant people" by Sir James Craig did nothing to dispel either Unionist pride in – or Nationalist alienation from – Northern

Ireland. In some Nationalist eyes the principles of justice, constitutional-ism and civic responsibility had been so corrupted that armed resistance could be supported, understood, tolerated and even on occasion excused to varying degrees. It should be noted, on the other hand, that Craig's famous phrase quoted above was a response to De Valera, the twenty-six county prime minister of the time, making reference to the Free State as "a Catholic state for a Catholic People".

The Republican struggle, was therefore, seen by Nationalists as a noble cause, even if many disagreed with the methods used in pursuit of that cause. Nationalists, although most of them abhorred violence, doubted that resistance to the "Unionist state" was either immoral or illegal and resisted the contention that Republicanism was a criminal venture.

That contention of Republican criminality was upheld by the Ulster Unionists, who had formed the Northern Ireland government from the inception of the state in 1921. They considered the enemy IRA as terrorists, pure and simple. The notion that the IRA could be fighting a just war was anathema to them. Moreover, many in the government considered that the Nationalist community's demand for civil rights was nothing more than a front for the IRA. From the Unionist point of view, Nationalists already had enough civil rights, so the notion that street demonstrations and marches were valid forms of protest was utterly contested by them.

The Northern Ireland government grew to consider their six-county Ulster to be a state under perpetual siege from Irish Nationalism. After all, the southern Irish government, that of the Free State, supported the IRA insurgency in Northern Ireland after partition, at least in Unionist eyes. While many Catholics would have viewed the IRA of that time as protect-ing them from intimidation and violence perpetrated by the overwhelm-ingly Protestant Royal Ulster Constabulary, B-Specials and other security forces, Unionists saw the IRA as a fifth column operating within its bor-ders, determined to bring down their cherished Northern Irish state.

Periodically after 1921, the Northern Ireland government warned of an IRA uprising and saw Nationalism as either being too sympathetic to Republicans (meaning the IRA and its radical Nationalist supporters), or worse, in cahoots with them. In 1937, De Valera published his new consti-tution for Ireland. In it, with the now famous Articles Two and Three, he asserted that the Ireland it referred was the whole thirty-two county island of Ireland – thereby claiming the Six Counties of Northern Ireland as part of his "national territory". To Unionists, this confirmed their worst fears;

that their southerly neighbour wanted to annex them and that the IRA was in the Six Counties to undermine the state-let and generally do De Valera's bidding.

To those Nationalists who bemoaned the lack of support for the IRA from the southern state, this was as preposterous to them as it was to the southern government – which at that time was imprisoning and executing IRA men more often than the British had ever done. Nevertheless, it was the raison d'etre of Irish Nationalism of all shades to undo partition, to end the state of Northern Ireland. In that sense, the Unionists were indeed under siege.

Their nerves were not soothed in 1949 when the south's Fine Gael/Clann na Poblachta coalition government declared Ireland a Republic, carefully leaving Articles Two and Three of the constitution intact. The British government responded by declaring that the status of Northern Ireland's position within the UK would not change without the consent of its inhabitants. To northern Republicans, this underlined Northern Ireland's inbuilt "Unionist veto", which ensured that constitutional change had no prospect of occurring via fair democratic means.

Tensions within Northern Ireland continued to grow. During the 1960s, anticipation of some IRA "offensive" became prevalent among Unionists and was at its highest around the time of the commemorations marking the fiftieth anniversary of the Easter Rising. Unionists were convinced that Nationalists would stop at nothing to take away their "Protestant country for a Protestant people". Nationalists came to realise that they would have to up their campaigning to achieve what they would consider real change.

Chapter Two:

Terrorists or soldiers?

In the late 1960s, with Northern Irish politics having hardened along sectarian lines, a movement among Catholic Nationalists against what they perceived as various infringements of their human rights by the Protestant establishment escalated into a two-pronged assault on the legitimacy of law and order in the north and, again, the validity of the Northern Irish state itself. On one hand was a peaceful political movement that began with a flurry of civil rights marches, while on the other were Republican Nationalists who felt peaceful politics could achieve nothing against what they saw as the establishment, the RUC and Unionist militants. Unionists certainly would have viewed events differently, seeing the protests as unnecessary or worse still, containing a hidden agenda; that is, an attempt to fatally wound the state itself. Unionists and Loyalists began to mobilise both figuratively and literally to protect the state. Republicans, pointing out that the civil-rights movement was powerless to defend itself against the violent backlash it soon provoked, looked at the precedents of history. If the Nationalist community wanted civil rights they would have to fight for it.

The initial response of the Unionist establishment to peaceful protests of the Northern Ireland Civil Rights Association (NICRA) beginning in 1968 against what they saw as discrimination in employment, housing and other issues, was to consider modest reforms. But to many Unionists the concessions from the Unionist government led by Capt Terence O'Neil, to the civil rights movement represented a "surrender to Popery" and a backlash followed. The fact that most Catholics saw the "reforms" as too little, too late illustrated the gap in perceptions. Many seminal events occurred around this period that became milestones on the road to the near civil war in Northern Ireland known as the "Troubles".

Between the "Battle of the Bogside" in 1968 (when the RUC confronted Catholics who had clashed with an Apprentice Boys parade as it passed the edge of the Nationalist Bogside area in Derry) and "Bloody Sunday" in 1972 (when British paratroopers shot dead fourteen unarmed civilians on a civil-rights march that had been declared illegal by William Faulkner's Unionist government of the time), Northern Ireland witnessed the emergence of the two IRAs: Officials and Provisionals, and two respective versions of the IRA's political wing, Sinn Fein.

This IRA split occurred in December 1969, with the breakaway group becoming known as the Provisional IRA. The "Provos" had, among other complaints, a conviction that the group they had left behind was too distracted by politics in general, and socialism in particular. The Provisional IRA felt that Catholics in Belfast had been left undefended during the violent backlash from Loyalists and the RUC that occurred through 1969. The Provos complained that there had been insufficient weaponry because the Official IRA had neglected its military responsibilities, and that notions of class struggle were irrelevant in a situation where Catholics were being burnt out of their homes – as had happened in Belfast.

Between 1969 and 1972, the paramilitary Loyalist UVF and UDA, along with the official security forces – the RUC, UDR and British Army, the latter deployed in August 1969 ostensibly to protect Catholic areas from Loyalist violence – were caught up in the backlash against the Catholic civil-rights movement. Some 700 lives were lost. The entire IRA, for their part, claimed to be defending the Catholic population from RUC and UDR brutality as well as from the murderous campaign of Loyalist paramilitaries. Loyalists insisted, however, that they were defending the Protestant people from an armed rebellion by the IRA who, they claimed, would stop at nothing short of a United Ireland. The RUC and Army had stated that they were "at war" with the IRA.

Nevertheless, the Unionist establishment and British government were at pains to stress that the IRA was not a warring army in any conventional sense, but an illegal organisation whose members were breaking the law. The IRA and its supporters saw their struggle in historic terms as a "war" against an unlawful and oppressive regime; the British and Unionists saw the IRA's actions as a "crime" against the state. To admit that the government was at war with the IRA would suggest to some, at home and abroad, that not only was the IRA a legitimate army but also that those members taken prisoner by the state of Northern Ireland should be treated as POWs. The government realised that the propaganda of such a scenario would boost the morale and support of the IRA, and so should be resisted at all costs. Notwithstanding such concerns, Chichester Clark, Prime Minister of Northern Ireland, had actually stated in February 1971 that his government was "at war with the IRA". This somewhat undermined the position of not according Republicans the status of soldiers.

The claim that IRA captives were POWs became an extremely sensitive issue for the British government, as a series of well-publicised human rights abuses against Nationalists and Republicans both inside and outside of captivity made the idea increasingly difficult to refute. With the world gripped by a "cold war" for the moral high ground between the Eastern communist power block of the Soviet Union and the Western capitalist block of the United States of America, the British – a key component of the Western block and its military wing, NATO – could ill afford to be portrayed as an abuser of human rights. Yet, by 1972, it was obvious to many outside observers that this was already happening.

Although the global aspect was of little interest to Unionists at that time, the security situation in Northern Ireland held a number of international propaganda perils for the British government. Bloody Sunday was itself disastrous enough in propaganda terms for the British, yet the fact that the marchers had been protesting against a security policy known as "Internment" created a further potential public-relations catastrophe for the government in London.

The British policy of Internment, introduced by the devolved Ulster Unionist government at Stormont in August 1971, was aimed from the outset exclusively at Catholics and Nationalists. A military swoop on entire neighbourhoods rounded up hundreds of Catholics, largely based on vague or out of date intelligence of involvement with IRA activities, who were then imprisoned without trial and subjected to a variety of punitive interrogation techniques. Internment had been preceded by the infamous Falls Road curfew of June 1970, when the British Army sealed of the Falls area of Belfast and conducted a house-to-house search for arms. Four people were killed by the army. The curfew was a last straw for those Catholics who had remained willing to believe that the army was there to protect them. They now regarded the army as simply an instrument of an oppressive Unionist regime, and support for the IRA grew.

Internment itself brought thousands of innocent Catholics face to face with the criminal justice system in the most pejorative sense possible. The initial swoop did not pick up a single Protestant, despite evidence of murders committed by Protestant Loyalist paramilitaries. Internment combined with Bloody Sunday to alienate and politicise a generation of Catholics – and further prepare the ideological and moral ground for the hunger strikes that lay ahead.

Writer and highly respected authority on the IRA, Tim Pat Coogan, sees Internment as indicative of a colonialist attitude among the British authorities towards the Irish – an attitude he believes has not entirely subsided. He also suggests that Internment demonstrated to Republican communities that the British security forces regarded them contemptuously as rebel colonials who were staging an uprising that had to be crushed by whatever means necessary. He further suggests the policy contributed to a hardening of attitudes on both sides – and left a resonance that remains eerily relevant to Britain's present "war on terror".

> You've got to remember that Internment turned the tide completely. Internment created a new breed. I mean civil rights was just out the window. Internment and related approaches came on the back of the Falls Road Curfew of June 1970. All this showed that the Brits and the Unionists believed in a military solution. This view was influenced by MI5, the Army and the RUC. MI6 would have had a more considered political view, I think.
>
> The impact [of Internment] was disastrous. They employed all these ghastly techniques, like filling a prisoner's ears with white noise; they hooded them and beat them senseless; they hooded them and pretended to throw them from helicopters. They employed all these colonial techniques, and all with the approval of the cabinet, who were briefed by Special Branch.
>
> I'll tell you when I first sensed a new brutality. There were three young Scottish soldiers killed by the IRA – two of them brothers – in their late teens, just. They were lured to a party supposedly, and while they got out the car to relieve themselves en route, the were shot dead. Now these brutal killings horrified Unionists, British and Irish, too. But there wasn't a mass outcry in Republican areas. They had seen the worst of the Army. The community's capacity to absorb such an event showed me that a huge escalation was taking place.
>
> Britain's Ambassador to Ireland at the time, John Peck, had that slightly colonial attitude. Very attentive, very cultivated. I said there should be dialogue with Republicans and that the propaganda should be discounted. The Brits were wrong. They were playing into the hands

of the physical force tradition; that tradition was becoming stronger as a result. He said London would think he'd "gone native".

Besides, many of the Army officers were naturally sympathetic to the Unionists. Many would have served in former colonies, like Kenya. They would have been of the view that "these people" were not ready for self-government. And the same would have been applied to these Irish rebels, as they would have seen them. There certainly was, and probably still is, a fair amount of anti-Irish feeling – a sort of condescending attitude among the mandarin class in England.

With hindsight, many on both sides of the debate today find it astonishing that Internment, so obviously an alienating factor and so clearly failing to stem the tide of violence, Republican or Unionist, was operated for so long – for four years, in fact. Not only that, but it was used as a bargaining chip by the British who presented it as a "concession" to Catholic Nationalists by replacing it with the "conveyor belt" system. This system introduced courts but no juries. This, the British argued, was necessary because of intimidation of juries by paramilitaries. A judge alone would determine the guilt of a defendant. In such circumstances, even after the introduction of the so-called conveyor belt, many Catholic Nationalists considered that the rule of law had been suspended. Unsurprisingly, the IRA flourished as many disaffected people thought that constitutional politics were not the answer. "The oldest debate," (between physical force Republicanism and peaceful means) as Tim Pat Coogan describes it, seemed to be swinging one way and one way only.

Condemnation of Britain's treatment of prisoners in Northern Ireland by its international enemies became a growing threat, as the Republican claim that Internees and other captives were POWs appeared to gain currency. Again, treatment of prisoners was seen in many countries as a test of a country's commitment to civil rights (and still is, witness the furore in Iraq over prisoner abuse allegations) and in the 1970s it was a constant criticism of the Soviet block by Western powers. The Soviet block had much to gain from turning the tide of criticism in the other direction.

However, the apparent ill-treatment of Republican and Nationalist prisoners meant that it was not only Britain's enemies who would be encouraged to take a special interest and "interfere in an internal UK matter". The United States of America, Britain's closest ally since the second world war, took a special interest in "Irish Affairs". The whole concept of Irishmen at war with Britain struck a chord with many of the forty million or so Americans who claimed Irish descent. The Irish had emigrated to the US for more than a century, prompted by such deprivations as the great potato famine and chronic poverty of the nineteenth century, and many, rightly or wrongly, blamed British rule for their enforced migration and the death of more than a million people during the famine.

The Irish lobby in the US – known as one of the "Three Is" that includes the equally formidable immigrant lobbies for Italy and Israel – has since become powerful to the extent that two of the last four US Presidents, Ronald Reagan and Bill Clinton, considered it politically expedient to claim Irish descent. Any US government mindful of the Irish-American lobby would have to have a policy on Northern Ireland. Some would argue that this policy would always be skewed since the Irish-American lobby, with its negative cultural memories of the history of British rule, was predisposed to be outraged by British actions in Northern Ireland and sympathetic towards the IRA. Where an imitate knowledge of actual contemporary events was not possessed, the "old knowledges" filled in the gaps, much to the annoyance of Ulster Unionists and successive British governments. Nevertheless, events such as Bloody Sunday prompted an outcry from the Irish-American lobby and forced the US government into taking a public position that, if not 100 per cent supportive of Irish concerns, at least voiced those concerns seriously.

In this context, the British government feared that such terms as POW or "political status", each with their resonance of American GIs in German prison camps and dissidents imprisoned in the Soviet block, would attract the wrong kind of attention from the Irish-American lobby in particular and from the US public generally. Conversely, the British also had to deal with an opposite set of sensitivities from the Unionists, for whom the term POW was also resonant of the Second World War – to them, the epitome of British fighting spirit and resistance. To accord such exalted status to an IRA that they saw killing woman and children in acts of terrorism, as Unionists saw it, was an insult to everything they believed about "war".

This debate over whether the IRA were terrorists or soldiers is pertinent to the Irish conflict from 1916 to the present day. It is a vital issue in relation to the 1981 hunger strikes and the British refusal to accord any status other than "criminal" to Republican prisoners. "Criminals" could not expect to gain support from a global audience, or even from Nationalists in Ireland who pursued their objective peacefully. Criminals would be dealt with by the law of the land and that was that, as far as the British and Unionists were concerned. If you wanted to achieve anything politically, so went this argument, then join or form a political party, contest elections and show everyone your mandate. After all, said the British, nobody would stop Republicans contesting elections but themselves. So any violent activity was criminal terrorism, full stop.

The policy of criminalisation was augmented, at various times and with varying degrees of emphasis, with "Ulsterisation" and "Normalisation". This three-pronged approach was forged into a coherent whole in the mid-1970s. The government planned the phasing out of Special Category Status, the replacement of Internment with the "conveyor-belt" system of "criminal" hearings and, the construction of the purpose-built containment facility at Long Kesh: the H-blocks. Eagerly pursued by the Thatcher administration in 1979 and during the hunger strikes, this policy was already well established – and not just in Ireland. Coogan again explains:

> The policy was "criminalisation", which sought to alienate the IRA from those supporting them, and "Ulsterisation", which sought to put local forces, both RUC and UDR, in the front line against IRA whilst British troops would offer support. This was also known as police primacy ... MI5 and MI6 would have been aware that this technique was used by colonial forces all over the world, by the British, by the Americans in Vietnam, where it had been called Vietnamisation. One attraction was that the local forces had local knowledge but also local prejudice. There was an awful lot of bias and ignorance. And then there was "normalisation", which sought to show that the IRA insurgency was having minimal effect on everyday life. This would encourage investment and at the same time show, as far as the British policy makers were concerned, that the lack of impact was due to the IRA's lack of support among it's own people.

The British were determined to hold this "criminalisation" line to discourage active and passive support for militant Republicans at home and abroad. They were determined to put daylight between the ordinary Nationalist population and the IRA, claiming that the "men of violence" represented nobody. However, events on the ground such as Bloody Sunday and other instances where British soldiers gave the impression of firing indiscriminately and resulting in the deaths of civilians, such as the barricade-clearing

Operation Motorman of 1972, simply brought many Nationalists to a position where, even if they could not support the IRA, then they couldn't support the British either. In a situation where Nationalists were being killed or imprisoned without trial by the state, while the state got away with what the Derry coroner described as "sheer unadulterated murder" (Bloody Sunday), the Catholic view of IRA prisoners was always going to be different from the British or Unionist view. This was not properly appreciated by successive British administrations and it seemed Britain had learned little from the time of the executions following the Easter Rising of 1916. It could be argued that criminalisation did not defeat the IRA. Rather, it generated support for Republicans.

The legitimacy of the Republican struggle was an article of faith for those in the Republican movement. To accept criminalisation, in their view, would be heresy and an insult to generations of comrades and family members who had resisted British and then Unionist rule – and to the concept of a reunited Ireland (it is easy for many in Britain to forget that Ireland ever was one country, so used are they now to hearing of "Northern Ireland"). To lose this battle against criminalisation would not only lose Republicans "the war" – it would mean the final defeat of the Republican soul, or so it felt to many. In this context, one can see why the hunger strikers, who had been radicalised by the convulsions of the 1960s and 70s, were committed to seeing their protest through to the death. It was more than their lives at stake – it was everything their communities believed in.

Chapter Three:

The hunger
for POW status

Out of the moral and ideological battle between criminalisation and POW status in the 1970s, hunger strikes would emerge in Britain's prison camps as the Republicans' weapon of choice. The IRA understood that hunger striking was a powerful means of asserting a prisoner's political legitimacy. The 1980-1 hunger strikers were not the first in modern Irish history; in fact, they drew much of their strength from the hunger strikers who had gone before them.

The capacity of hunger strikes to disrupt attempts by the British state to criminalize its internal political enemies had been felt not only in Ireland, but in Britain too. From 1909 to 1914, the British Suffragette movement, which campaigned for the vote for women, resorted to the weapon of hunger strike and it became one of their most potent – although not for the same reasons as it did in Ireland in 1981. It wasn't the death of Suffragette hunger strikers that gave this weapon its power. It was the force-feeding policy with which the British responded, provoking outcry and increased support for the Suffragettes. Once details of the brutality of force-feeding became public, the authorities were in a no-win situation. For forced feeding is one of only two responses that authorities intent on facing down a hunger strike can use. The other option, of course, is to let the hunger striker die. Either way, the hunger striker is on the way to martyrdom by degrees.

While the Suffragettes could not state with certainty that their hunger strikes won the vote for woman, the resulting force-feeding and the sympathy it earned them did their cause no harm – a fact that did not go unnoticed. It was in Ireland itself, however, that the use of hunger strikes as a political weapon would really come into its own. During the early twentieth century, hundreds of Republicans – men and women – would go on hunger strike to be recognised as POWs.

In Ireland in 1913, James Connolly, the Scottish-born leader of the Irish Citizens Army and soon to be one of the leaders of the Easter Rising in Dublin, went on hunger strike while in prison for attending meetings "inciting sedition" (supporting a trade union in a labour dispute). Fortunately for the authorities, he was released a week later, ensuring a long battle of wills was avoided. Given the determination Connolly demonstrated in events surrounding the Irish revolution, one can guess he would have gone to the grave if need be.

Another of the most famous Republican hunger strikes was that of Thomas Ashe in 1917. The impact of Ashe's death has many parallels with that of the death of Sands 64 years later. Ashe was the president of the Irish Republican Brotherhood, a component part of the Irish Volunteers and forerunner of the IRA. In Ireland in 1917 there was a great fear of conscription being introduced for the British Army. Ireland was in no mood to die for Britain and even "moderate" Nationalists were against conscription. Many spoke out against it. Ashe, however, was arrested for this (as were others) and charged with sedition. He was sentenced to two years' imprisonment. The Irish penal authorities of the day had no legal means of differentiating Ashe and other Nationalist prisoners from common criminals. In a chilling forerunner of future events, Ashe refused to do prison work or wear prison clothes. A hunger strike was organised in support of free association (thus invoking three of the five POW demands that the 1980-1 hunger strikers in the H-blocks would later make), and Ashe was on it. There was a feeling that the British government, which controlled Irish jails, would not let him die. After all, the government's reaction to the Easter Rising, executing fifteen captured rebels, had ensured the Rising had more support than would have otherwise been the case. And the force-feeding of the suffragettes had won the government no friends. Surely the British had learned from such events?

Only five days after the strike started, however, Ashe died from being force-fed. When the details of the coroner's report were disseminated in the press, the impact of such a brutal measure engendered outrage among an already outraged population. Riding on the back of the Easter Rising executions and conscription, the manner of Ashe's death attracted more than 40,000 mourners in Dublin alone, with events in sympathy arranged all over Ireland. The death of this hunger striker united IRB, Irish National Volunteers (the more moderate grouping loyal to Redmond, the Irish Parliamentary Party leader) and the Irish Volunteers (Eoin McNeill's faction that had broken away from the main grouping). Armed volunteers formed a guard of honour and most of the events nationwide were organised by Sinn Fein.

The experience of this organising, coupled with the electioneering Sinn Fein had been involved with since 1916, consolidated Sinn Fein as a political force. The sympathy generated by Ashe's death ensured that this force could draw on more support than ever before. This was further consolidated when the prison authorities told the prisoners after nine days of the strike (four days after Ashe's death) that the government had granted POW status. Far from being satisfied, many Irishmen were bitter that Ashe had to die in the first place if what he sought was offered now. So the government managed to get the worst of both worlds. They inspired a revolutionary movement with Sinn Fein in the vanguard – and they conceded to the demands of that movement's prisoners. All eerily familiar with the 1980-1 strikes and their aftermath.

Political status won by Ashe's strike, a victory consolidated by further mass strikes in April 1920 by IRA prisoners, was withdrawn by the British in October of that year, as they sought ways to discourage Irish support during the Tan War (another name for the twenty-six county War of Independence). This reversal simply produced yet another martyr for the Republican cause when Terrence MacSwiney, Sinn Fein Lord Mayor of Cork City and Commandant Cork Brigade of the IRA was allowed to die in Brixton jail, England, on October 25 after seventy-four days on hunger strike. It was the third death from hunger striking that month, Michael Fitzgerald dying on October 17 and Joseph Murphy dying just a few hours before MacSwiney. Once again, far from discouraging the IRA, this merely hardened their resolve and increased their support among the general Irish population.

Whether immediately successful or not, hunger strikes used in pursuit of a cause that was well supported were a mighty strong stick to beat any government with. In fact, after the Free State was created and the government was therefore an Irish Republican one (made up of those Republicans who accepted the treaty that partitioned Ireland) the anti-treaty IRA used the tactic against it. At one point, there were 7,000 IRA prisoners on hunger strike demanding political status, four of whom died between June 1923 and December 1923 – Dan Downey, Joe Witty, Denis Barry and Andrew Sullivan.

In 1940, with the Second World War consuming Europe but De Valera's

Ireland remaining neutral, members of the anti-treaty IRA were still active, being arrested and serving jail terms in the Free State – almost twenty years after the treaty. In April 1940, Tony D'Arcy from Galway died after fifty-two days on hunger strike for political status. Three days later, Sean McNeela joined him after fifty-five days on strike. Six years later, after a twenty-three day fast, Sean McCaughey also died (he'd also given up water after 16 days, hence his rapid descent). All died in Irish Free State jails.

The first member of the Provisional IRA to die on hunger strike was Michael Gaughan, in the spring of 1974. From Ballina, Co Mayo, he left Ireland for England in search of work, where he joined the IRA. After being convicted of firearms offences, and serving time in Wormwood Scrubs and Albany Prison, where Gaughan requested political status, he was transferred to Parkhurst prison. There, four other IRA members (Marion and Dolores Price, Hugh Feeney and Gerry Kelly) were already on hunger strike for political status. Since 1972 such status had been partly granted as "Special Category Status", but only in Northern Ireland – not in the rest of the UK. On March 31 1974, Gaughan joined the strike. British policy at this time was to force-feed hunger strikers. Six to eight guards would restrain the prisoner and drag him or her by the hair to the top of the bed, where they would stretch the prisoner's neck over the metal rail, force a block between their teeth and pass a feeding tube, which extended down the throat, through a hole in the block. The process would leave the prisoner bruised and carried the danger of the tube passing into the lungs rather than into the stomach. The last time Gaughan endured this procedure was on June 2, 1974. The next day he died, aged 24, from injuries inflicted by force-feeding. He had been on hunger strike for 67 days.

Fellow IRA member and Mayo man, Frank Stagg, was the next hunger striker to die for political status. He had been arrested in England the previous year and was convicted of arson-related offences. He had also been ordered off a previous hunger strike, the same one in which Gaughan died, after 68 days. 18 months later, he went on another hunger strike, his fourth. This time, he was on strike not for political status as such, but to be transferred to Ireland. In February 1976, after 62 days on hunger strike at Wakefield prison, he died.

Stagg's death produced some notorious footnotes. Instead of arriving at Dublin airport, where his family had gathered in wait, the flight carrying Stagg's body had been secretly diverted to Shannon airport in the west of Ireland. It was then transferred by the Irish authorities to Ballina, Co

Mayo, and buried in concrete by the Gardai under the instructions of the Irish Fine Gael/Labour coalition of the time. One night, nine months later, Republicans tunnelled into the concrete, collected Stagg's remains and re-buried them in the Republican plot.

As we can see, the demand for political status was nothing new in 1980-1. The British, however, at the start of the Troubles had concluded that POW status, or any political status, was asking for trouble. They believed that potential "terrorists" would be encouraged join the IRA and take part in violent acts if they thought that they would not serve time as a criminal and, secondly, there was some sort of status on offer. The British saw political status as a reward for violence. This raises the question of why the British did concede, temporarily, partial recognition of POW status to the IRA in 1972 in response to a hunger strike. Had a hunger strike succeeded in forcing the British authorities to recognise the legitimacy of the Republican cause in Northern Ireland?

Chapter Four:

'Special' status won and lost

In the wake of Bloody Sunday and the backlash against Internment, Ted Heath, the Tory British Prime Minister, decided that the devolved Northern Irish parliament at Stormont was incapable of containing the spiralling security crisis. On March 24, Heath informed Stormont that control of security including the RUC would be transferred to London. The response from Faulkner and his colleagues in the Unionist administration was to walk out, and Stormont was suspended by Westminster.

Not long thereafter, Heath appointed William Whitelaw as Secretary of State for Northern Ireland with a status brief similar to that of a colonial governor. Whitelaw was supported by the Northern Ireland Office (NIO), which performed most of the executive functions previously undertaken by Faulkner's Unionists. A new constitutional arrangement was sought and discussions with the southern Irish government, the Unionists and northern Nationalists over the following eighteen months culminated in the Sunningdale Agreement. This agreement instituted a power-sharing formula acceptable to a slim majority of Unionists (a majority that lasted only a few months) and the majority of northern Nationalists.

While the discussions for a new constitutional arrangement were taking place in the summer of 1972, Whitelaw met the Provisional IRA in secret in July to discuss a possible ceasefire that would help take the heat out of the security situation. The Official IRA, whose fighting effectiveness had been reduced after the split with the Provisionals robbed them of many of their best military talents, had wound up their military operations in May. Before agreeing to meet Whitelaw, the Provisional IRA laid down certain preconditions. Since May 15, Billy McKee, the Provisional IRA's officer commanding (OC) in Belfast until his arrest in 1971, had been on hunger strike in

Crumlin Road prison, Belfast, for POW status. One of the IRA's preconditions was that McKee's demand for political status be granted. Whitelaw was intrigued by the possibility of a ceasefire, although he publicly claimed he wouldn't meet the "terrorists". He was attracted not only by the obvious benefits it would bring to the streets, but also to his burgeoning political initiatives. He eventually agreed, after being persuaded by the SDLP's John Hume and Paddy Devlin, to meet the IRA.

The IRA called a ceasefire to show Whitelaw that it was a disciplined army and on June 19, 1972, Whitelaw created "Special Category Status", which applied to all prisoners convicted of Troubles-related offences. Whitelaw would later deeply regret this politically expedient move, calling it one of his biggest mistakes of his long political career. Some considered that the civil disturbance that occurred in response to a rumour McKee had died on hunger strike influenced Whitelaw. Nevertheless, on June 22, the IRA announced a ceasefire to run for seven days from June 26 – a potential first step towards a complete end to its armed campaign.

There were, however, elements within the British security establishment that were appalled at Whitelaw's decision to offer the IRA de facto POW status. Later that year, in November, the British Army conceded that personnel from its Military Reconnaissance Force (MRF) had shot and killed civilians during this ceasefire. The British used weapons recovered from Republicans to do so, and their intention was to undermine the IRA ceasefire. To some in the security services, Special Category Status meant that a political solution rather than a military solution was being sought. This would deprive those who wanted nothing other than the defeat and surrender of the IRA the victory they were determined to have.

Nevertheless, the new policy was implemented. It enabled both Republican and Loyalists paramilitary groupings to organise themselves in prison, mainly at Long Kesh, in wartime Nissen Huts that created the impression of POW camp. Prisoners could wear their own clothes, have free association, arrange their own educational and recreational activities, and did not have to do prison work. This was a major step indeed, as far as the history of Republican prisoners is concerned. The demands of many hunger strikers, many of whom had died over the years, had been met by the British government. The new status only applied in Northern Ireland, however, not in England.

The British perhaps felt that some kind of compromise on the prison issue was necessary and could even be beneficial in the propaganda war. While this notion would be at variance with previous British concerns regarding granting POW status, time had moved on. With anger at Internment refusing to subside, particularly with stories of torture and beatings emanating from released internees – often backed up by medical evidence – this gesture of goodwill on the part of the British might have been perceived by some to contradict IRA propaganda. Besides, it was not genuine POW status, it was "Special Category Status". Nonetheless the conditions effected were those sought by Republican prisoners, regardless of what face-saving name was given to them. The intelligence value of the internees was greater than the propaganda value relating to "political status" and in a climate where the British felt the need to be seen to be flexible, then the latter was marginally more dispensable than the former. It was, in any analysis, a gamble – one that the prize of a ceasefire made worth taking

The ceasefire, however, broke down during a dispute over relocating Catholics into houses vacated by Protestants in the Lenadoon area of Belfast. Some would contend that elements within the army were determined to see it break down. But the British were left with the reality of "Special Category Status", political status in all but name. They knew this status was of value to the IRA and so could be used as a bargaining chip in any negotiations, not that Whitelaw or the Conservatives had any intention of directly negotiating with the IRA again, deeming their demands for a ceasefire (immediate withdrawal of all troops and a statement declaring reunification of Ireland within five years, for example) as being unrealistic and un-negotiable.

The British focused on the negotiations with all willing constitutional parties that later resulted in the Sunningdale Agreement, and the power-sharing executive of 1974. These were concluded without Republicans, who saw Sunningdale as an irrelevance as it was not the thirty-two county Irish Republic they were fighting for. The IRA and Loyalist paramilitaries continued their campaign and the death toll in the conflict rose each year, polarising the communities as each side visited horror on the other. The army and RUC were also responsible for a large number of deaths, further convincing many that any war against them was just and indeed a "war". Special Category Status, whether a good thing or a bad thing, certainly did have the effect of encouraging participants and their supporters to believe that they would not, if caught and jailed, be treated as criminals. Since Special Category Status had been granted, the death toll had nearly doubled. There were many factors involved in that increase, however, and it is debatable whether Special Category Status had any discernable or direct impact on these figures at all. However, opponents of the policy within the new Labour government of Harold Wilson, elected at the general election of February 1974, and among Unionists, would stress the apparent link between the granting of special recognition and the rise in casualties.

The new Labour government commissioned a study of how Britain should deal with the IRA effectively, without infringing the human rights of the Nationalist people generally and the prisoners specifically. The Gardiner committee reported in January 1975 and recommended the ending of Special Category Status. It also came close to recommending the end of Internment, stating that while effective in the short term: " ... the effects of the use of detention are ultimately inimical to community life, fan a widespread sense of grievance and injustice, and obstruct those elements in Northern Ireland society which could lead to reconciliation ... "

However, the report said it was a matter for the government to make such a "grave" decision. Nevertheless, the government saw an opportunity to get themselves off the Internment hook, which was causing them more embarrassment every month it was in place. Cases of those imprisoned without trial were being taken up by human rights lawyers and protests against it were made in the US and the UK on a regular basis. Add to this the fact that Britain was implementing a new policy of "Ulsterisation", which meant the RUC would take over many of the roles performed by the British Army, and therefore be at the forefront of security efforts directed primarily against the IRA. The cynics noted that this would mean less British soldiers being sent home in coffins, lessening the political damage Northern Ireland was causing to the government.

The ending of Internment and the implementation of Ulsterisation were essential planks in an overall move towards "normalisation", itself a policy designed to present an image to the world that Northern Ireland was an everyday society, not one at war. In addition to IRA violence, Loyalist paramilitaries were killing Catholics at a terrifying rate, ensuring that the IRA were supported by some sections of the community as a protection force. The British and Unionists (and many Nationalist commentators, such as Malachy O'Docherty many years later) contested the notion of the IRA as a "protective force", suggesting that IRA actions endangered the lives of more Catholics than they protected. Republicans would point out that without the IRA, the Unionists, British Army, RUC and B-Specials would all have had a free run. As well as actually resisting incursions of Loyalists into

Nationalist areas (such as at St Matthew's Church, Short Strand, 1970), many Republicans considered the IRA as much a deterrent force as anything else.

Merlyn Rees, the Labour government's Secretary of State for Northern Ireland, implemented suggestions made in the Gardiner Report and decided to end Special Category Status. He also confirmed that he would phase out Internment, having announced that intention in April 1974. He stated that as of March 1, 1976, anyone convicted thereafter would not be entitled to special status and would not serve their time in the compounds of Long Kesh. They would instead be imprisoned in the Maze/Long Kesh, a purpose built state-of-the-art prison with eight blocks built in the shape of an "H", hence the term "H-blocks". Prisoners convicted prior to this date would serve out their time in the Long Kesh compounds, under Special Category Status.

The British knew there was no way the Republicans would accept this but they had ceased to consider Republicans as part of the solution, viewing them instead as part of the problem. They believed they could isolate "unrepresentative gunmen" politically when the benefits of "normalisation" became apparent to all. The government were focused on defeating the IRA militarily. The SAS were brought into Northern Ireland as the government took the fight to Republicans and, when Roy Mason succeeded Rees as Northern Ireland Secretary in September 1976, he made it clear that he intended to "squeeze the IRA like a tube of toothpaste".

Prior to Mason taking office, some seminal events took place out of public view. Some in the security services, especially within MI6, had, over the years, come to the view that "killing the IRA with kindness" was the surest way to end the insurgency. By this they did not mean being soft on "terrorism", but rather focusing on taking away the perceived need among Catholics for the IRA to exist. On Special Category Status, some in MI6 believed it was best not to "tinker" with it, believing the propaganda harvest for the IRA would outweigh any benefits. One source familiar with MI6 thinking had this to say:

> They did not doubt that the IRA could be beaten. Their instincts were to do all they could to bring that about militarily, once and for all. MI6 knew Ireland well, and knew its history well. They were sure that the army had the capability to win, as long as their efforts were targeted precisely against the IRA, not the wider Nationalist or Republican community. But, very quickly, things would go wrong. Civilians were killed, recklessly in their view. Nobody was brought to account and

the army's response lost them the trust of Catholics. Yes, you could defeat the IRA, but in the process, you'd create the next IRA. It may take twenty, thirty, even fifty years, but they would always come back while the Nationalists felt alienated from the state.

Partition was essential to protect the British minority on Ireland. But that minority had ballsed up the governance of Northern Ireland so much that a third of the population hated the place as much as they did fifty years before. One could say that the IRA was beaten in Northern Ireland by the 1940s – and the 50s campaign achieved nothing. And yet, here they were in 1972, stronger than ever. To avoid a repetition of that scenario, some felt that a more far-sighted approach was necessary. This was not to appease the IRA, who committed dreadful crimes. It was to end violence. That was why the IRA were engaged behind the scenes. It resulted in a ceasefire in 1972 and again in 1975. The latter ceasefire came after Protestant clergy met the IRA in the aftermath of the Birmingham pub bombings. It would be naive to suppose, however, that MI6 played no part in facilitating this. One consideration was Special Category Status in Long Kesh. MI6 knew Rees was constantly being badgered by the Unionists to do away with it, for obvious reasons. There were many in the NIO, too, who gave such advice. The people I'm thinking of advised to keep it in place for the moment.

So according to this account, some in MI6 were considering a "political" strategy, though there is plenty of evidence in the public domain to suggest that this was by no means to the exclusion of more military methods. They were no peaceniks. The Wilson government was not popular with any of Britain's secret services, as has been well documented, yet those with "political" inclinations within MI6 and the Wilson government both agreed on the need to at least explore a political solution. It was hoped that by legalising Sinn Fein, as was done in 1974, politically minded Republicans would be encouraged to pursue their agenda without guns. It was one of a series of moves presented by the Wilson government as offering a long-term alternative to armed struggle, while also meeting the government's short-term objective of an IRA ceasefire.

There are, however, those both on the Republican and British sides who have suggested that this ceasefire was not what the British actually wanted. What the British were really playing for, some believe, was victory over the IRA. Even the "doves" in the intelligence agencies wanted nothing less. The ceasefire was, suggested some contributors for this book, a disingenuous ruse to tempt the enemy out into the open, and then render them ineffective. This would "encourage" the development of political methods once the hopelessness of military ones became apparent to the leadership of Provisional IRA.

It was not only Republicans that MI6 had to consider. The rivalries between the various security services have been well documented, and it is suffice to say here that many in MI5 did not share what they considered the cautious analysis of some in MI6. Some in MI5 believed, as did the regular British Army, that the IRA was very close to defeat. Now was the time to hit them on all fronts. Disastrous IRA bombings that killed civilians were losing them support among the Nationalist community. The IRA themselves were, according to intelligence analysis, losing the hearts and minds of Catholics. This process saw a consolidation of support for the "moderate" Nationalist party, the SDLP, and in so far as the security services had any influence, this was not discouraged. The SDLP was the political option that should be encouraged, not Sinn Fein, who had been made legal against the advice of some in MI5. Special Category Status had to go. It muddied the waters, MI5 argued, by giving credence to the notion that Republicans were political when they had not yet reached that point, at least not to the satisfaction of the British. The long-standing concept of "criminalisation" received renewed impetus around this time and its adherents became an ever louder voice in the ears of British ministers.

So the IRA's year-long ceasefire from February 10 1975 to January 23 1976, while seeming to validate the analysis of some in MI6 that political progress was possible, was an unwelcome distraction for those in MI5 who were determined to defeat the IRA militarily. While Gardiner was reporting that Special Category Status should be reconsidered, the government had not yet decided when it might implement such a policy. The ceasefire was of value to the British at this time, as was demonstrated by the government developing contacts with Sinn Fein. Sinn Fein set up, with the government's backing, incident centres to monitor the ceasefire and look into any breaches of it. Fears among Unionists that a British announcement to withdraw was in the offing were high. With hindsight, this seems highly unlikely to have been seriously considered but, nevertheless, Loyalist paramilitaries felt the need to increase their killing rate dramatically to provoke the IRA. The vast majority of their victims were civilians, some tortured and murdered by the Shankill Butchers gang.

The Loyalists and elements in MI5 had a shared enemy and a shared objective – the end of the ceasefire. Both wanted the IRA defeated and both hated the Wilson government. It seems unlikely in the face of all the recent evidence regarding collusion between British intelligence and known Loyalist death squads, that two organisations with shared aims remained incommunicado throughout a period many of them considered an "emergency". Many of the Loyalists involved in sectarian killings were agents run by various strands of the security services, including MI5. It has been alleged by several books that the security services did not only turn a blind eye to many activities but allegedly instigated or facilitated some of them The ceasefire was instantly under strain from many factors, most prominently the sectarian war that engulfed parts of Belfast and County Armagh. Some would suggest the advent of this war was "fortuitous", to say the very least, for MI5.

Whether or not collusion played a part, those elements in the security services whose ultimate objective was to defeat the IRA also wanted to bring about the termination of special status for IRA prisoners as a matter of urgency. As long as special status and the 1975 ceasefire were in operation, they believed, the British government would be prone to following the political path to peace rather than the military road to victory.

Over the course of 1975, elements in MI5 worked against MI6 having any influence in Northern Ireland and, according to some, by the end of that year, they had almost achieved this. This did not bode well for the development of political strategies that could reach out to Republicans. Nor did it bode well for the prisoners. Politicians base their decisions on Northern Ireland on intelligence briefings to a large degree, and Rees was now receiving advice from sources who did not want the IRA to develop politically. With the deaths of so many soldiers, policemen and civilians at the hands of the IRA, it might be surprising if the army had taken any other position. Republicans point out that "everybody suffered in the conflict" but it was the army and MI5 who were painting the picture for Rees.

Some accounts of the Troubles suggest that Rees was, in any case, never serious about developing political links with Republicans. It might be less contentious to suggest that Rees did not impose his will on the Six Counties, and often chose the path of least resistance, perhaps not wanting to make a bad situation worse. A source familiar with intelligence thinking on Ireland at that time suggests:

Some people thought the minister could be influenced by events. So, some people endeavoured to shape events in a particular way. Most of the British military wanted to finish the job. They considered the political option was a means of getting the IRA off the hook. They did not trust Republicans. They thought they'd start again when they did not get their own way. Some in the intelligence community had a slightly different slant.

They usually had some notions about Labour governments being bad for Britain. Handing the IRA respectability on a plate undermined the global view of Britain. You'd imagine that would be MI6's concern. But MI5 were concerned about a lot of things. Let's say Republicans had grasped politics and abandoned armed struggle at this time. The Labour Party would have had a major policy success. That was bad for MI5. The IRA would have a political voice and have, therefore, some influence in Northern Ireland. That was bad for MI5. The only thing good for MI5, as far as I could see, was the continuance of the IRA campaign until the IRA was totally annihilated. They saw the SAS as the answer. They believed that the army had one hand tied behind their back for political considerations. The SAS would not have had that concern.

The success of MI5 in presenting its case ensured political initiatives such as Special Category Status were finished. With MI5 now in overall control of security policy on the ground, all theatres of "war" would feel the effects. Republicans in South Armagh and other Republican strongholds would feel the change in the field, as the SAS were introduced (prior to this they had been engaged in Northern Ireland under various guises, such as "Four Field Survey Troop" and other tags). And captive Republicans would feel the change as the prison policy moved in tandem with policy on the outside. In January 1976, Rees announced the ending of Special Category Status. The IRA ceasefire collapsed into a sea of sectarian violence, notably in Armagh, where at Kingsmills an IRA unit using the cover name of the Republican Action Force shot dead ten Protestants in cold blood in retaliation for the murder of seven Catholics by the UVF in the preceding days. Republicans were demoralised by the failure of the ceasefire. They had been compromised by British intelligence and informers and interrogation techniques ensured that they were being squeezed from both ends. Just as Lloyd-George had done during the War of Independence, the British really did feel now that they "had terror by the throat". But, just as in 1921, things didn't quite work out that way.

Chapter Five:

Blanketmen

On September 14, 1976, Kieran Nugent was given three years for hijacking a lorry by a Diplock court. He was the first Republican prisoner to be sentences after the ending of Special Category Status. Diplock courts were the name given to the conveyor-belt process of trying "scheduled offences", what the IRA termed political offences, in front of three judges. Supporters of this process claimed it was necessary as juries were susceptible to intimidation by paramilitaries. Opponents countered that it was just another way of ensuring more convictions without evidence. Diplock courts were an integral part of the government's renewed "criminalisation" policy.

As the first IRA man to be sentenced after the withdrawal of Special Category Status, Nugent was required to wear prison uniform. He famously told the warden who tried to issue him with his uniform that he would have to "nail it to my back". Later, when he was put in his H-block cell, he was given a blanket, as all prisoners were. He used this, instead of a prison uniform, to cover himself. In doing so, he became the first "Blanketman". Many more would follow, as hundreds of Republican prisoners refused to wear prison uniforms.

Going "on the blanket" was not a form of protest for the fainthearted. Prisoners would have no reading material, no furniture of any kind and, obviously, no clothes. A mattress was provided, but only at night. During the day, it was taken out. Going on the blanket did not just mean obvious physical privations but, as not wearing prison uniform was an infringement of the rules, the protest incurred additional penalties such as loss of remission (temporary or early release). It also incurred the wrath of prison officers who were not well disposed to Republican inmates at the best of times, never mind when they were breaking the rules and protesting.

Many expected the protest to peter out in due course. Instead, more and more prisoners joined it. There were more than 250 prisoners on the blanket by the middle of 1978 (and more than 500 by 1980). It soon became clear that the prisoners were not going to back down. The authorities, for their part, saw no reason to back down either as they held all the cards. As far as Secretary Of State for Northern Ireland, Roy Mason and the NIO were concerned, they had the IRA close to being beaten. There was no doubt the new security policies were having an effect and would do what MI5 had suggested they could do along provided they were implemented as intended; that is, without what they saw as 'kid gloves'. Mason had regular security meetings with RUC Chief Constable Kenneth Newman and the GOC of the army in Ireland. With the military side proceeding almost to plan, Mason sensed a historic opportunity to smash the IRA.

That opportunity would be diminished by the Republican campaign to generate support for the prison protests among the wider Nationalist community. Before the days of the internet, it was not as easy then as it is now to spread information quickly, or even at all. The public at large became aware of the protest through determined efforts by the families of prisoners, although it wasn't until August 1978 that the National H-block Campaign committee was formed. Prior to that, many Republican activists were assisting the families of prisoners (who had formed Relatives Action Committees) but the lack of a national campaign indicated just how much work Republicans had to do to become an effective campaigning force, never mind develop a political party.

The activities of this time, based on two core issues of the conditions in which prisoners were held and the demand for the return of special status were to prove extremely durable. Gradually, momentum gathered around the relatives' campaign as the consciousness of the Nationalist population as a whole was awoken. Even those who opposed the methods of the IRA, some from an ideological abhorrence of all violence and some from fear of the legal consequences, could campaign for better conditions for the prisoners on what they saw as humanitarian grounds. The images that eventually made it into the public domain of the Blanketmen evoked suffering. Their hair and beards were long. To the vast majority of Catholics, the symbolism of such suffering was obvious.

To combat the Blanketmen campaign, the southern Irish government banned the voices of Sinn Fein representatives being aired in the Republic and initially, outside Republican or family circles, few seemed to know or care what was going on. The authorities were convinced that the campaign, both outside and inside the prison, was being manipulated by the IRA leadership. In reality, the leadership did not need to manipulate prisoners who had already joined the IRA knowing that death or imprisonment were the two most likely options. They believed they were not joining a criminal organisation but a guerrilla movement that had been founded over 60 years before, itself built on a tradition of resistance to British rule over hundreds of years. With that inbuilt commitment, many Republican prisoners needed little if any encouragement to protest against the taking away of what they considered the most basic right of Republican prisoners, POW status. Once the protest was established, backing down was not an option and many of these men would go for years dressed only in their blanket.

Contrary to the authorities' suspicions, the IRA leadership were uneasy about the protests. They could not be seen to be doing anything other than supporting them, but they remained unconvinced convinced that such protests would win the support of the wider Nationalist population. And, if no support was forthcoming, it would be demoralising for the prisoners, their families and the Republican community. The IRA did not share the British view that militarily they were beaten. The still had a "war" to fight and damaging sideshows could turn into fatal distractions. They had indeed come close to defeat. The 1975 ceasefire had all disadvantages of the 1920 ceasefire that had been faced by the IRA of Michael Collins. Once the fighting was over, IRA men were more visible, off their guard. The organisation was easier to monitor and easier to infiltrate. The IRA had around 1500 active volunteers in 1975/76. Not prosecuting their war was disorientating for them. The security forces were therefore well positioned to take advantage of the situation when the ceasefire broke down. It was this that led Mason and his successor, Humphrey Atkins, who took his post when the Conservatives won the UK general election of 1979, to believe that the military solution (as opposed to the political solution) was just around the corner.

However, the British did not realise the extent to which the IRA had recognised these weaknesses and begun reorganising on a model prescribed by many of those who had been in jail during the ceasefire, including Gerry Adams. These Republicans had not been involved in agreeing the ceasefire so, as far as IRA rank and file were concerned, their hands were clean – the ceasefire by now having been accepted by most of the IRA as a near-fatal error. The IRA was streamlined. Instead of the quasi-military model of companies and battalions, they shrunk into active service units (ASUs) of small groups of trusted people. Not everyone in an ASU would know who the other members were. This made them difficult to penetrate and harder to monitor. Much more emphasis was put on planning operations and, over the two-year period of 1977-79, the IRA had quietly been getting its act together. It was in this context that the IRA did not want a distracting protest, though they understood it was a just one, to muddy the waters. The prisoners, however, had to be supported.

In fact, when the blanket protest resulted in a further deterioration in prisoners' rights and a lack of positive action by the government it was added to by another resistance tactic – the dirty or no-wash protest – in 1978. After prisoners were harassed and beaten by prison staff as they went to the toilets, they refused to leave their cells and so used their cell buckets to relieve themselves into. Staff then ceased to bring buckets, forcing the prisoners to smear their own excreta on the walls of their cells to dispose of the waste. Tim Pat Coogan, one of the first authors to write about the Blanketmen and the prison protests, recalls that amid the extraordinary stoicism and irreverence of the protesters was the sheer horror of what the protest actually entailed:

> I remember going to see Martin Meehan [an IRA prisoner] who was in the blocks at the time on the blanket. There he was in his cell, all Christ-like with his white towel round him. I remember I thought he looked like a boxer. And on the cell walls, were these patterns drawn in the shite that was smeared on them. And he was drawing palm trees, and he said: "This is a map of the Pacific."

At first, the fears of the outside leadership that prison protests were an unhelpful distraction appeared well founded. The campaign to raise awareness was not high profile at this time and little apparent progress was made. The prisoners themselves were writing to everyone they could think of; politicians and Church leaders in the UK, US, EEC, UN, and all over the world, trying to make people aware of the conditions they were imprisoned in and why POW status should be reinstated. As writing materials were banned from the protesting prisoners, these letters were smuggled out the H-blocks in "comms".

Comms were communications written in tiny writing on cigarette papers, toilet paper and anything the prisoners could get to write on. These comms were then concealed intimately about the person and exchanged when prisoners met with relatives once a month. As only one meeting per month was allowed per prisoner, the leadership inside the H-blocks would organise the rotation of these visits to ensure the maximum number of communications possible. Protesting prisoners were not allowed any visits by the authorities, so selected prisoners wore the uniform that one day a month when they were on "visiting duty". As the prisoners were searched before and after each visit, the comms had to be concealed imaginatively, to say the least. They were hidden in mouths, anuses, foreskins of penises and anywhere else that could be utilised.

It wasn't just comms that were smuggled. Prisoners built makeshift radio sets from smuggled parts. The ingenuity of the prisoners knew no bounds and most things that were deemed necessary found their way inside the H-blocks. In this way, communication with the leadership outside was enabled. During the hunger strikes to come, this line of communication was a lifeline for Republicans.

Despite these efforts, the campaigning relatives groups were the only pressure groups initially taking up the prisoners' case. Some in the IRA considered this potentially distracting, though they could not say so. The SDLP considered the whole episode embarrassing and a poor reflection on Catholics. The Church saw it as none of their business and the press imposed self-censorship. For instance, the editor-in-chief of the Sunday Observer, Conor Cruise O'Brien, tried to sack the Observer's Irish correspondent, Mary Holland, because of the way she wrote up an interview with the mother of an H-block prisoner, making it quite clear that he objected to anything that might arouse sympathy for the prisoners. And this was not an uncommon position, ironically, in the south of Ireland. RTE did not want to cover the protest at all. They ignored the protests.

The prisoners' campaign therefore had to consist of writing letters to every important person they could think of, in an attempt to raise awareness of their conditions. Reaction to these letters varied from indifference to hostility and the prisoners were discouraged at times. Eventually, the Catholic Church began to take an interest. One of the high-profile figures who would take an interest in the prisoners' plight was the then Catholic Primate of Ireland, Cardinal Tomás Ó Fiaich, who would play a sympathetic if equivocal role in the struggle that followed. But the general response from people in high places was unsympathetic.

The prisoners still wrote to relatives, as they were forming Relatives Action Committees (RACs), Turf Lodge being one of the first. Since 1976, the prisoners had realised that they had to co-ordinate their activities if the campaign was to grow. The RACs that sprang up all over Ireland were the nucleus of a national campaign, which the prisoners decided early on to tap into in a more organised manner.

Reproduced below is a historic document. It is the first joint letter from the prisoners signed by their newly appointed press officer, Richard McAuley. The letter sets the tone of the new arrangement as the prisoners give instructions to the relatives, utilising them as an auxiliary force. This is perhaps an example of the Provisional IRA getting involved in "non-military" campaigning. The act of becoming involved in this "political" activity was an eye-opener for many Republicans who wondered if this could be pursued. It became the first step for some militant Republicans on their road to politics.

Republican POW Letter to RACs
REPUBLICAN PRISONERS OF WAR
LONG KESH CONCENTRATION CAMP
MONDAY 22 NOV 1976
TO RELATIVE ACTION GROUPS: ALL AREAS

A Chara,

This is the first opportunity in quite a while for the Press Relations Officer to write to you directly on the subject of political status for sentenced prisoners of war. Until now it has been the practice for the prisoners themselves to write and communicate with their particular area committee and this will remain the case, apart from this one instance. I have a few points for your approval, but before raising them I would like, on behalf of all the prisoners from all areas, to offer you our sincere thanks for the sterling work you have carried out to date. This never was an easy task, but the drive and determination of the area committees in getting the message across has been an inspiration to us all and we take great succour from your efforts. Such worthwhile success will ensure that we will not lose the issue at hand – of that we are supremely confident. There is still a long way to go and there are many hardships to bear, but your committee and the many like it will sustain the men behind the wire and in the cellblocks until that victory is won – and won it will be.

You will be aware of the fact that the numbers of men in the cell blocks grow daily, and that further repressive measures have been taken by the NIO and the prison staff against the prisoners in a desperate attempt to break them and have them conform to the status of criminal. Proudly and defiantly, the prisoners are resisting these attempts by the prison staff and the NIO and, although naked and in solitary confinement, they have voiced their determination never to allow themselves to be treated as criminals. Mass has now been denied the men and they are not even allowed out of their cells to empty their chamber pots unless they go in prison clothes to do so. Exercise is now also denied them men and they are locked up 24 hours per day, with no contact with another living person. The eye looking through the peep-hole in the cell door is the only sign of life they see outside of meal times, when their meals are shoved through a gap in the door – as would be seen any day during feeding time for the animals at Belle Veu Zoo. Despite these disgusting methods, the men are not broken and their morale is high as ever, befitting the cause for which they are imprisoned and belying the criminal tag the NIO are trying to place upon them.

Now that it is clearly obvious that the NIO are escalating their campaign against the helpless prisoners, we believe it is time we in turn escalate our support for the men. There are various ways this can be done, and some are listed below. It is of course obvious that not every area can apply every one of the suggestions, but those who can do should begin as quickly as possible in conjunction with the Central Committee (who have been furnished with a copy of these proposals) and all other active groups in your immediate vicinity. The proposals are as follows:

(1) The continuation and escalation of the protest rallies and meetings to highlight the plight of the prisoners

(2) The circulation of a petition form asking signatories to support the stand for status. These petition forms should be printed by the Central Committee, who would collect them completed, for presentation to the NIO after a period of four weeks. Copies of the petition form should be printed in the Republican News, An Phoblacht, Andersonstown News, and all local news sheets for four successive weeks. The forms should be on display outside all chapels at every mass and devotions for the four-week period, and be available at all rallies and protests.

(3) Everyone should be encouraged to ring the NIO at Dundonald 4522 (Treatment of Offenders Branch) and register with them their

support for the prisoners. This was done earlier in the year and was very successful in that the switchboards at the NIO were jammed for considerable periods.

(4) Pickets at Council Offices where meetings are scheduled or in progress (country areas). Letters to the Councils are also effective in that they are read as part of Council business and therefore are generally reported in the provincial press.

(5) Pickets and sit-ins at travel agencies and Government Dept Buildings, with banners, petition forms on display. Numbers at such pickets need not be great and effective sit-ins have been lodged with only ten protesters present.

(6) Protests outside prisons and courthouses, especially when prisoners are on trial.

(7) Blocking of main roads and junctions by women with prams, again a very effective means of protest which generally gets coverage in the media, especially where women accompanied by children make up the bulk of the protesters.

(8) Poster campaigns. New and graphic posters are this moment being designed for distribution to all areas and these will be available within the next few weeks. Area committees should ensure that these are placed in every available shop and house in the area.

Those then are just some of the ideas your area might find practical. As mentioned earlier we are circulating these ideas to all areas and to the Central Committee for their approval. It would be hoped that this new phase would be launched in early December and carry through to January, reaching a pitch at Christmas – a time of great stress for the men in the cell blocks, and a time when it can be calculated with extreme confidence that the NIO will apply even more repressive measures against the prisoners to try to break them. We have established a means by which the prisoners in the cellblocks can learn of the support actions being taken on their behalf. For them it will be a lean and bleak Christmas but at least they will have the knowledge that it is not all one-sided and that there are those on the outside who are enough to raise their voices in protest, defeating the British intention of tagging our men as criminals. The men in the cellblocks are the only true Irishmen; off their knees and openly defiant of the British and their ways.

Again, may I offer on behalf of these men our sincere thanks and appreciation for all you have done in the past for this most noble of causes. We wish you, your Committee, and all your families, the Happiest and Holiest of Christmases. Our prayers will be with you and will be offered for your intentions.

Is Mise,
R.G. McAuley, PRO

Chapter Six:

Activists reactivated

The non-violent and dignified nature of the Blanketmen protest had the effect of re-engaging a large constituency of community activists who had become alienated from the Republicans' armed struggle not only by some dubious IRA operations but the sheer volume of blood spilled in every direction during the 1970s. In doing so, the blanket protest paved the way for the induction of this crucial civilian support network into the hunger strike campaign – a campaign that emerged when it became clear the blanket and other protests needed to be augmented with something more potent.

Some observers would contend that the apparent reorienting of Republican tactics towards political protest, suggesting a desire to seek alternatives to armed struggle where possible, triggered a "latent Republicanism" in the broader Nationalist psyche. It is argued that this Republicanism had lain dormant in many Nationalists' minds since partition, when it became clear that, in their view, they were trapped in a Unionist state. Apart from a brief flurry of Republican election successes in the mid-1950s, when four Sinn Fein representatives were elected on abstentionist tickets in the south of Ireland and two in the north (both Republican prisoners), there had not been a real Republican electoral option for Nationalists to vote for. That said, Republicans in the 1953 Stormont election had done well, and one of their successful candidates, Liam Kelly of Pomeroy, had stated during his campaign that he believed in physical force – "the more the better".

When arms were taken up shortly thereafter, support, while initially strong, soon waned. The failure of the IRA 'Border' campaign of 1956-62 to garner significant backing from the Nationalist community, combined with the limited reforms and relative liberalisation under Northern Ireland Prime Minister Terence O'Neil from 1963 to 1969, suggested to many Nationalists that a constitutional approach was the realistic political option. The Nationalist Party re-entered Northern Ireland's parliament at Stormont in 1965 and relations between the governments of both jurisdictions on the island thawed considerably, demonstrated by Taoiseach Sean Leamas, a veteran of the 1916 Easter Rising, arriving in Belfast for talks with O'Neil. Although this meeting was fiercely opposed by such figures as the Reverend Ian Paisley, who represented the feelings of those Unionists opposed to O'Neil's reforms by throwing snowballs at Leamas's car as it left Stormont, there was a sense among many of a new situation for Nationalists.

When it became clear that O'Neil had lost the battle for Unionism's soul, a defeat manifested in the belligerent rejection of his policies by such hardliners as Paisley, as well as losing the support of elements in his own party, Nationalists realised that they had to force the pace of change. The campaign for social justice and civil rights from 1964 onwards, intended to keep the agenda of reform and liberalisation on track, provoked a furious response from Unionists. The resultant disturbances, riots and general disorder brought Northern Ireland to what O'Neil famously stated was its "crossroads".

As the situation deteriorated, a new Nationalist party was formed in 1970 to try to further social justice by peaceful political means. The Social Democratic and Labour Party (SDLP) was led by Belfast's Republican Labour MP, Gerry Fitt, and also contained future leader Derry's John Hume. In the wake of what many Nationalists refer to as the pogroms in Belfast and other areas, with many thousands of Catholics (and some Protestants too) forced to leave their homes in the biggest forced movement of civilians in Europe since the second world war, some northern Republicans, perceiving the IRA of neglecting its duty of protecting Catholic areas at the height of this tumultuous time, had split and formed the Provisional IRA and Provisional Sinn Fein. Unlike the SDLP, this new Republican movement was clearly not a constitutional one and, apart from a few local instances, Sinn Fein would refuse to contest elections throughout the 1970s. Republicans believed the situation required a non-constitutional approach focused on defending Catholic areas, consolidating a power base and then going on the offensive for the only solution they believed would ultimately guarantee Nationalists their rights (and their safety): the reunification of Ireland.

Nationalists were left with only one real constitutional political party to vote for, the SDLP. Many SDLP voters had varying degrees of sympathy for some form of Republicanism; many other Catholics simply didn't vote, perceiving the SDLP as not addressing their political aspirations. There were other reasons why potential Republican voters either abstained or voted for the SDLP. While the actions of Loyalists, the RUC and the British Army appalled many Nationalists, so to did IRA operations that went wrong, like Bloody Friday (1972), La Mons (1978) and others where large numbers of civilians were killed. Contrary to British reports of the time and since, the IRA did not set out to kill civilians on these operations and most Republicans, while accepting such casualties as inevitable in war (and James Chichester-Clarke had declared that his Northern Irish government "was at war with the IRA") were similarly appalled at such tragedies. Many sympathisers would have questioned whether this was an organisation to which they could give unqualified support. But that did not mean they ceased to understand why organisations such as the IRA existed. And such an understanding ensured that this constituency remained suspicious of British and Unionists attempts to criminalize Republicans.

The new, non-violent plank of resistance to the criminalisation of prisoners, developed during the blanket protest and later the hunger strikes, allowed the IRA to tap into this dormant well of Republican (perhaps "Republican" with a small "r") sentiment among the Nationalist community. As community activists became more involved, some Republicans remember the RACs gradually morphing into the H-block committees under the direction of the National H-block Committee, founded on October 21, 1979, at a meeting in the Andersonstown area of west Belfast. Sometimes relatives stayed on and became political, and they were joined by Sinn Fein and other Republican activists who gradually took control. Of course, some of these activists were already relatives themselves. Johnny Donaghy, a Republican activist and brother of Tom Donaghy, an IRA prisoner from south Derry (later murdered in 1991 by Loyalists working in conjunction with British agents, an example of "Collusion"), remembers the impact of the blanket protests and the prisoners' thinking that lead to the hunger strikes, which in turn had an explosive effect on a hitherto slow-stirring public support. He describes vividly the prevailing atmosphere of the time:

> I had sort of dropped out the movement for a while ... during 1978 in fact. A good friend of mine, a good volunteer, was executed by the IRA and I disagreed very strongly with that. I had dropped out of the movement for a time over this as had many others in this area ... Well, despite having left, the hunger strikes, indeed the whole blanket protest, caused me to get re-involved and I have been ever since. I can think of

many others who did the same, you know, for one reason or another they had dropped out but the hunger strikes brought many people back into the movement. And they came back more committed than before and so embittering an experience were the hunger strikes that most have never thought of leaving since, no matter what else they experienced afterwards. That experience was repeated throughout Ireland, but particularly in the North.

Galvanised by the experience of the hunger strikes, the mechanism that had initially brought Donaghy himself back into the Republican fold had been a local Relatives Action Committee set up to support the blanket protest. He recalls:

I remember Mrs Betty Noone and others being active in setting up a local Relatives Action Committee in the area. People had been concerned about the conditions that the prisoners were enduring in Long Kesh. Some were relatives, some were Republicans. But everyone was sort of acting independently of each other. The Relative Action Committees were a way of bringing everything together more, of acting cohesively. We'd plan where to protest and think of the ways of protesting that would have an effect. People like John Davey [Chairman of South Derry Sinn Fein] later shot dead by the UVF, Kevin Agnew, Hugh Corey [who had a son on the blanket], the Neesons, Terence McGonigle and others were instrumental at that time. So what started as a loose collection of people became a wee force of people, purely to gain support for the prisoners. We were trying to highlight the prisoners' conditions. The protests didn't have a very high profile at all at first. In fact, I remember one protest in 1978 and it seemed like we were outnumbered by the RUC by twenty to one.

We knew it was only a matter of time before a hunger strike was coming. We had talked to the POWs and seen comms telling us, and two POWs had already died on hunger strike in English prisons. We knew we had to convince people that this was what would happen if there were no improvements in conditions at Long Kesh. Unless they were affected themselves, people maybe didn't really believe just how bad things were. And in the H-blocks, things were particularly bad. People just didn't seem to think that things would come to a hunger strike.

Many of us, though, had relatives on the blanket. We were seeing conditions for ourselves on a weekly or monthly visit, depending on the visits. I think some people not directly affected might have seen us slightly as "fanatics", or not quite on the same level, because we had this personal interest. But to me, the hunger strikes changed that. People saw us coming up against the British Army and the RUC, in all weathers, seven nights a week. And they thought, if they can do it, so can we. People would know each other as neighbours and through Sinn Fein, the GAA and things like that. Support sort of snowballed from that. John Davey was someone who did everything possible for the prisoners, and the hunger strikers in particular, short of going on hunger strike himself. He organised, he marched, he protested – along with many others, of course. I'm sure there were nights that man never went to bed.

Now during the first hunger strike [of December 1980] support was growing. We saw that ourselves. And after the prisoners were tricked out of the hunger strike, attitudes around here hardened. This swung them right behind the second strike.

There were prisoners from south Derry on hunger strike. And people knew that they weren't terrorists. They were their friends and neighbours. So nothing the Brits said about them would change people's minds about them. And they wanted the Brits to let them live.

Another thing was that there was a certain number of us, actually a large number of us, who were regularly harassed by the RUC, the Army and the UDR. But it didn't stop us protesting. Again, because others saw this and because attitudes were hardening, people thought, well, if they can take it, so can we. As well as this, a lot of people would have supported Republican aims but would have had a problem with the methods being used to achieve them, or perhaps they would have seen the movement as an elitist group where they had no place. The H-block committees were easier to join, and then people would discover that they had a place and a part to play.

Many of those protesting formed the foundation of the modern [Sinn Fein] party. They were stalwarts who stayed the course. Some were ex-prisoners. I'd say there would have been about eighty to 100 hardcore activists in every town and village about here at that time, and that number could double or triple according to the different stages in the hunger strike. Some families got it really hard, The McGlincheys from Bellaghy were one example. I think there was about five of them went through the prisons. And there were seven of our family went through; brother, cousins, uncle, nephew. And that process was repeated all over the North. There were large extended families all with direct experience of people either in prison or out protesting. And then you consider their friends, and their neighbours … I think the Brits underestimated the number of people actually affected by the whole system.

During 1980-1, when the blanket protest gave birth to the hunger strikes, the number of people affected or who felt the need to get involved grew. During the second hunger strike, led by Sands, each time a hunger striker died it became a focal point for protests – but also for conflict between the security forces and Nationalists, resulting in more Nationalists being brutalised and jailed. Donaghy recalls:

The day Bobby Sands died, we organised a protest at Drumagarner near Kilrea. There was a van full of police which had been watching us all morning and, as we crossed the road, it drove straight into us. It hit two of us – I remember thinking they were trying to kill us. The RUC, the UDR or the Brits could isolate you at anytime, out on the roads, for questioning. You could be at their mercy for an hour or more, with a gun held to your neck. I remember our Tom telling me that after he was arrested in 1977, the interrogation was the worst ever. They could easily have killed you. One interrogator told him that they could kill a detainee in Castlereagh and be in less trouble [with their superiors] than if they released him; they said this had already happened twice.

Behind their intensive campaign to portray such events as a struggle between the forces of "law and order" and supporters of the "criminal" IRA, the British government did not appreciate that while many unaffected directly could be influenced by media claims and political pressure, there was a growing rump of support for militant Republicanism that was aware of a completely different IRA from the one portrayed by British propaganda. This was a more human IRA, whose members won admiration and active support from neighbours for exploits that seemed to be acts of resistance against British soldiers and RUC personnel whose behaviour in these areas instilled loathing. Even among their enemies, such Republicans won grudging respect. Donaghy recalls:

I remember reading an article by one British Army officer who'd been stationed in south Derry referring to the IRA men on the run in this area as Ireland's equivalent of the SAS, in the way that they were living off the land, sleeping out, and the way they went about things.

Conversely, when attempting to portray such men as terrorists, the British did not appreciate that the perception of their own forces in areas such as south Derry was often one of contempt.

Some of the soldiers you'd maybe have a bit of respect for. I suppose there were some elements of the British Army that did not seem to be going out their way to get at you. Some of them were fellas doing a job. Not the SAS, though. They were a gang of murderers who would be only brought in here to execute Republicans. And many people in the DMSU [the RUC's Divisional Mobile Support Units] were the same – they were used to implement the shoot-to-kill policy, assassinating Republicans in highly dubious circumstances

Such perceptions sustained the Republican core support base. With the hunger strikes and the protests that preceded and then accompanied them, this support base grew from the die-hards to more and more everyday Nationalists who were not convinced the IRA were terrorists, and who saw the British government's intransigence in dealing with the hunger strikers as unnecessarily brutal. The response of security forces to protesting Republicans was witnessed by ordinary people who felt themselves identifying more and more with their friends, relatives and neighbours. In this way, politicisation of the general Nationalist people occurred. This does not mean they all became Republicans overnight, or at all. Many still supported the SDLP and many either condemned, or at least were extremely uncomfortable with, physical force. But they also condemned the attitude of the government which was, in the opinion of Nationalists, if not provoking, then at least prolonging the prison crisis.

Moreover, having witnessed the fierce response of the security forces to what they considered peaceful protest, many considered the government's attitude to violence an exercise in double standards. The families, neighbours and friends of prisoners were not just affected by the conditions of prisoners and the resulting protests, but also by more sinister developments. Donaghy recalls:

Ex-prisoners were targeted, murdered by the Brits. So were many on the H-block committees. The Brits sought out ones they realised had leadership qualities. They executed a number of local Republicans who would have had potential. They were taking out local leadership. It was clear-cut collusion. I believe, generally, elements of the UDR would have scouted out the area and then Loyalists or the army came in.

Eamples of how this process worked are illustrated in these recollections of a later period.

Later on there were two attempts on my life. One of them I am ninety-nine per cent sure was attempted by the security forces. Three of us were in a field ... when about seven shots from a high velocity rifle just missed us. Whoever fired them was a good shot. They fired from a good distance and were shooting to kill. He'd rested the rifle on the roof of a car. The car was later traced to a member of the security forces. We never reported the incident. But the next day there was a British Army unit out at the scene asking who'd been shot. They were told that no-one had been shot. They said that they were sure someone was. They were sneering and laughing as they asked.

The second occasion was a couple of fellas on a motorbike. There had been members of the security forces around quite a few times earlier. Then there was someone asking directions, asking me did I know such and such a house number. I said, 'who are you looking for?' He said he didn't know. Later on, the bike came by and I heard the pillion passenger shouting, 'That's the house, that's him'. I'd been on my guard, though, and got back inside. My nephew had been shot and survived shortly before this incident, and my brother Tom had been shot dead in August 1991. My uncle had survived three murder attempts and there had been clear evidence of collusion in all these incidents.

The same system was nearly always repeated each time, with a massive security force presence for several weeks scouting about and then disappearing just before the actual killing. This happened in the case of twelve Republicans and four Nationalist civilians who were murdered in this area of south Derry and North Antrim over the years. As well as this, there were about five more attempted or aborted murder attempts we were aware of.

Despite facing the realities of renewed state terror, Republican activists like Donaghy were galvanised by the determination of the Blanketmen and, especially, the hunger strikers' sacrifice. A new generation was being swept into the struggle by a tidal wave of moral compulsion, although human nature meant that some elements picked up by the tide would inevitably create new problems as the movement expanded in the years that followed. Donaghy concludes:

> The hunger strikers drew a lot of admiration. These were selfless acts. No matter what, there was no getting away from the courage of the thing. And of course, as well as returning Republicans, the movement had a whole new generation of activists, of volunteers. A new generation of touts as well – any influx will have a mixture of good and bad.

Chapter Seven:

'Let's see what politics can do'

If the resurgent Republican activism out on the streets was to be transformed into a mass movement with an international profile, it was recognised by some that the prison protests of the late 1970s and 80s would have to be bolted to a new semi-constitutional strategy of contesting elections – the successful outcome of which could have a huge impact on the standing of the Republican movement. Although initially there was no grand scheme to move towards constitutional methods, it was recognised by some that by contesting and winning elections as POWs, the prisoners could trigger a massive leap forward.

A consequence of this organically developing line of political thought was that Sands was subsequently elected to Westminster and Doherty and Agnew to the Dail. For the first time, the modern IRA – the Provisional IRA – would test itself at the ballot box with Republican prisoners standing as H-block candidates, as it had been challenged to do by many for some time. Their victories were to confound the belief held in Britain and around the world that the prisoners' had no support. When the elected Sands paid the ultimate price for his protest in 1981, 100,000 people would attend his funeral on May 7. The British could call it misguided support, the Unionists could call it insulting support; but it was undeniably support. It demonstrated that an essential component in the British profile of Irish Republicanism was flawed.

Yet it very nearly didn't happen. The fact that these elections were to be contested at all was a major break from previous Republican strategy, and many were decidedly against the move. The risks for the Republican movement were great. If Sands were to lose the Fermanagh-South Tyrone by-election of April 9, 1981, it could prove a fatal blow to morale. The subsequent history of the Troubles and the electoral fate of Sinn Fein would certainly have been very different. So what prompted Republicans to take such an internally contentious and politically risky step?

The answer lies in the re-evaluation of the struggle's direction that had been taking place inside and outside prison over the preceding years. Seanna Walsh, who was officer commanding (OC) of the Provisional IRA prisoners in The H-blocks when he was released in 2000 as part of the Belfast Agreement, had also been an OC in the H-blocks at the time of the hunger strikes. He had known Sands and was highly respected by the Republican prisoners. Indeed, when the IRA released a DVD in July 2005 instructing volunteers to dump arms, the man who read out the order was Seanna Walsh. Walsh, like many other Republicans back in the 1970s, was initially sceptical of electoral ventures. However, as a result of discussion over a period of time, he was to play a part in persuading others to "see what politics could do". He recalls:

> The hunger strikes challenged the perception that the prisoners were criminals. Would criminals lay down their lives? If it hadn't been for the situation in the north of Ireland at the time, these people wouldn't have been in jail. This was after the civil rights protest and the marches, and so on. After Bloody Sunday, people thought, well, what's the point in marching now?
>
> When Frank Maguire [the independent Republican Westminster MP in the Fermanagh-South Tyrone constituency] died, Republicans thought, "well, just maybe". The thinking was, let's give politics the chance to prove itself. Prior to that we would have thought, "so what if we win an election?" The Brits will still be here. And the whole point was to get them out, whatever it took. They'd still be here, and they'd still have to be beat, no matter what elections we might have won. Also, Republicans were convinced that the British could corrupt any election process, with their propaganda and media control. We original-ly thought, OK – politics could run parallel to the struggle to a degree, but not if they became a distraction. There was a fear that we could be sidetracked. Even when Bernadette [Devlin McAliskey] ran on an anti-H-block ticket in the Euro elections of 1979, a lot of Republicans were against that at the time. Some Republicans would have thought that all our attention should be focused on the war, on the military aspects. So the electoral debates were formulated then. When Bobby won many did

think, perhaps there is another way. The hunger strikes and the support they brought about helped Republicans establish a bridgehead as far as politics were concerned.

While Bernadette Devlin McAliskey won just under 34,000 votes, considered a respectable performance at a time when expectations were low, her campaign was actively opposed by some prominent Republicans – even though she was campaigning on behalf of the prisoners. Although she was initially encouraged by many relatives of some Blanketmen, and by senior Sinn Fein figures in Dublin, she was fiercely criticised by many northern Republicans for entering the fray. There was even a statement from prisoners that physical force was all the British would ever respond to.

Some campaigners from that era suggest that McAliskey might have polled more votes had the entire Republican movement supported her. McAliskey makes the point that standing was an issue, but it was about protecting prisoners' rights, improving their conditions and pursuing their claim to political status. There was no grand plan at this stage in the minds of most anti-H Block supporters to build a constitutional political party.

Prior to the crisis in the prisons, McAliskey, as Unity candidate, had been elected to Westminster as an MP by winning the Mid Ulster by-election of 1969. She was re-elected at the general election of the following year, but lost the seat in the February 1974 election. McAliskey had helped organise the defence of the Bogside area of Derry in 1969 after its residents resisted RUC attempts to enter it (the incident that became known as the Battle of the Bogside). She had earlier come to prominence as a member of the student group, People's Democracy, which campaigned for civil rights alongside such figures as Hume and Fitt in NICRA.

In 1974, McAliskey became a founder member of the Irish Republican Socialist Party (IRSP). She later left the IRSP and, in the late 70s, helped organise protests on behalf of Republican prisoners. At that time, around 300 were "on the blanket". Like many high-profile members of the National H-block Committee she was shot, along with her husband, by Loyalist gunmen (in this case, the UFF) at her Co Tyrone home on January 16, 1981. Allegations of dirty tricks surrounded what was a clearly co-ordinated campaign to assassinate the leaders of the H-block protests. In this case, troops were said to have had the house under surveillance at the time of the shooting and were immediately on the scene. A soldier gave McAliskey first aid, perhaps saving her life. However, the question remained: why had the

attack gone ahead if the house was surrounded with troops? Someone somewhere was obviously determined that those assisting the prisoner protests
should either be killed or intimidated out of action. This perhaps indicates
the importance that was attached to the prisoner protests by those ordering
the killings.

Badly wounded, McAliskey miraculously survived. Some of her colleagues on the committee were not so lucky. She'd famously described legendary Co Derry IRA and then INLA man, Dominic McGlinchey, at his
funeral, as "the greatest Republican of them all". Nevertheless, McAliskey
remained a committed Republican and went on to oppose the Republican
ceasefire in 1994 that helped pave the way for Sinn Fein's lurching rise to
power in the 1990s, saying: "The good guys have lost". It is with some irony
that McAliskey remembers Sinn Fein opposition to her pro-prisoners campaign in the Euro election of 1979:

> When we were first organising the support rallies for the prisoners,
> Sinn Fein weren't interested. They didn't want to get involved. For us,
> though, in the rural areas of Tyrone, it was a question of supporting
> the prisoners. We were doing it instinctively. We were doing what came
> naturally to us, and we weren't going to be dictated to by anybody.
> When I wanted to stand for election there was opposition to that, and
> of course Sinn Fein advised people to boycott the vote and by implica-
> tion boycott the vote for me – even though I was standing on a pro-
> prisoners platform. After the results of the vote were announced, it was
> clear that we had tapped into a huge vein of support and that people
> were clearly interested in coming out and supporting the prisoners.
>
> Sinn Fein realised this and it was then that they became interested
> in becoming involved. You have to put Sinn Fein in context at this
> time, though. In the late 1970s, Sinn Fein was a talking shop. Being
> a member of it was almost looked down upon by other Republicans.
> They thought it was the soft option to join it. I remember one meeting
> in Tyrone that we called to discuss ways to support the prisoners. In
> walked Sinn Fein and a couple of local Republicans. The Sinn Fein guy
> was from Belfast and he started trying to dictate to us what we could
> and couldn't do. We just laughed at him. There was no way some up-
> start from Belfast was going to come down to us and tell us how to run
> the campaign. We went on about our business – but we always left the
> door open for Sinn Fein. If they wanted to come and join us they could,

and eventually, of course, they did. But it must be made clear that at the start of the campaign, they didn't want to know about it. Maybe it was because of their dogmatic approach to not contesting elections – an approach they have completely abandoned in recent times, of course, but they were against it at the time.

In addition to any dogmatic concerns about abstaining from elections, there was, as Seanna Walsh points out, a genuine fear of electioneering competing for resources and focus with the armed struggle – just at the moment when it was beginning to regain its own momentum. In fact, 1979 in some ways threatened or promised (depending on your point of view) a resurgent IRA. As we have seen, the Provisionals had restructured themselves into small cells, making it harder for the intelligence services and the army to penetrate.

The blueprint for this new IRA had been constructed in cages at Long Kesh by several young Republicans including Ivor Bell, Danny Morrison, Sands and others led by Gerry Adams. These prisoners and others formed a think-tank, which concluded that the ceasefire of 1974-75 had been a disaster which nearly defeated the IRA. They felt the then leadership of O'Conaill and O'Bradiagh had been lured into trap and so these Young Turks planned to revamp the movement militarily. They were also convinced that the movement had been penetrated by reasonably high-ranking informers. Indeed, they realised that they had been arrested as a result of an informer whose identity they worked out together in jail. So they considered it imperative that the IRA be restructured. These men also formed the view that they were best placed to lead the movement into a new era. To get support from volunteers, the best way was to show that they could deliver weaponry and show that a resumed military campaign could make an impact. And, as some commentators have pointed out, "politics" was, to many at that time, a dirty word.

By 1979, IRA operations seemed to encourage the belief that it had recovered. The volunteers were better armed than before, and the operation at Narrow Water, where eighteen paratroopers were killed in an well-planned ambush, combined with the assassination of Lord Mountbatten in his boat off the Sligo coast (including four civilians in the boat with him) convinced some Republicans that they could once again advance against the British militarily.

In 1978, a report by Brigadier James Glover of the British Army had fallen into IRA hands. In it, Glover conceded that the IRA could not be beaten and that its present volunteers were not unemployable thugs but actually dedicated, experienced and competent insurgents who would not be defeated militarily in the foreseeable future. The report was not intended to be defeatist from a British point of view. It simply was at pains to show the British administration and those in the army charged with defeating the IRA, that they had to realistic about "taking on terrorism". They had to know the scale of the task to have a chance of succeeding. Talking tough about defeating the IRA might lead politicians to look a bit ridiculous should these basic facts not be acknowledged in any British analysis. Also, the IRA's new blueprint had fallen into the hands of the Irish security forces, and therefore into British hands as well, when Seamus Twoomey – an IRA army council member on the run in the south of Ireland at the time – was arrested in Dublin with a copy in his possession.

Both the British and the Republican volunteers were aware that the Provisional IRA was still a formidable opponent to the British in Ireland. Morale among some volunteers was rising, so it would be easy to see why electoral politics did not captivate all of them at this time. The question is, what changed their minds? Seanna Walsh again:

> Well, there came a time when some of us thought, right, let's see what politics can do. You have to remember that we had been protesting since 1976, when political status had been done away with. We'd had the blanket protest and then the dirty protest for years, and nothing had changed. We were also suffering daily abuse from the screws.
>
> Hunger strike had been considered an option since the end of political status. Billy McKee had won political status with a hunger strike in 1972. It was always an option. But, for obvious reasons, we were reluctant to go on it right away. At the end of the 1980 hunger strike [led by then H-block OC, Brendan Hughes] the bones of a deal were there. Some in England advised compromise but the NIO scuppered the deal by threatening to resign en masse if any concessions were made. The mentality of most of those in the NIO at the time was a laager mentality. After the second series of hunger strikes were over, the demands were granted by stealth. So what a shame ten men had to die in the first place. But then probably we wouldn't be in this position now.

One possible interpretation, then, is that Republicans felt they had little to lose by contending an election at this stage after years of protest in the prisons – including protests by Republican prisoners in the women's prison at Armagh. Contesting the election could be seen as a logical escalation of the protests that preceded it; blanket, no-wash, hunger strike, then election. So perhaps it wasn't a rash gamble. Republicans were sure there was a significant support base. Their campaign could not have continued to this point without it. It was how to consolidate and build on this base that had exercised minds, even before the prison protest came to prominence.

While public sympathy for the prisoners, even among Nationalists, was hard to maintain prior to the hunger strike, the core could always be relied upon. In the days before Provisional Sinn Fein was the mass party it is today, this dependable core of highly motivated and uniquely committed activists would campaign for Republicans. Also, the National H-block Committee and Relatives Action Committees had gained experience of campaigning over a number of years for the prisoners' political status. Some Republicans speculated that, regardless of what support levels for the prisoners appeared to be initially, should a hunger striker was chosen as a candidate for an election, then that level of support would surely rise. While these factors did not eliminate the risks attached to contesting elections, they were considerable arguments in favour of 'giving politics a chance'.

Chapter Eight:

Combatants in a new struggle

While the debate regarding electoral contests and other forms of politics continued, the decision was taken to ramp up the prison protests and build a more high-profile campaign. The first phase took place in October 1980, when seven selected volunteers (six IRA, one INLA) went fifty-three days without food to demand political status. The strike was eventually called off on the understanding that it had secured agreed concessions from the British government. The rapid deterioration of one of the hunger strikers, Sean McKenna, had presented a deadly dilemma to Brendan Hughes, the leader of the strike, who had no choice but to take the proposals on trust, or let McKenna die, perhaps unnecessarily. That 'offer' later turned out to be not what it appeared (or was reneged on) and therefore set the scene for the second hunger strike led by Sands. Research for this book has confirmed from two separate British sources that the document grudgingly accepted in the desperate circumstances of McKenna's deterioration was indeed designed to trick Republicans into coming off their hunger strike – and in such a way that the government could claim it was a defeat for the IRA.

One of the 1980 hunger strikers was Tommy McKearney, a member of The Provisional IRA. He was arrested in 1977 and sentenced to life imprisonment in the H-blocks. Released from Long Kesh in 1993, McKearney now works with ex-prisoners and with the Independent Workers Union in Ireland. He is known for his independent thinking and is highly respected within Republican circles. McKearney remembers the parliamentary politics debate within the movement during 1980-1. He recalls:

> At that time, the IRA was re-evaluating its options. Introducing Parliamentary politics was always going to be a sensitive issue, given

the history of the IRA from around the 1969/70 split. So, the idea of contesting elections and other methods of struggle would have to be dripped slowly if it was going to actually get through. The election of Bobby Sands sustained the argument that elections were worth contesting. His election was demonstrable proof that we could progress in an electoral contest and so show that we had support for the struggle.

As to the notion that the IRA was at this stage a resurgent military organisation, with its restructuring and morale boosting military successes such as Warrenpoint presenting an obstacle to more constitutional thinking, McKearney reveals that Republicans knew they needed to develop a more comprehensive, long-term political strategy:

These [military successes] were blips on an otherwise downward trajectory. The re-evaluation was necessary. By the late 70s it was clear that the military campaign was not really bearing fruit. A lot of the old assumptions had to go and we realised that we were in for a long haul. It was no longer like 'Victory in 73' for instance.

We had to consider what the options were. There could be a continuation of armed struggle. That was obviously one option. Then there was the political route – or I should say the parliamentary political route. By that I mean we'd always been political. Shooting a soldier – that's a political act. It was parliamentary politics that was a specifically discussed. And then there was what I'd say was a third option. I hesitate to use the term "a third way"

Like many socialists, McKearney considers the term "third way" to carry pejorative connotations of duplicity and fraudulence relating to the rightward shift of socialist and social democratic politics generally in the 1980s and 1990s, yet by the same token it also mirrors the concern within the Republican and Nationalists movements that a path which was neither pure armed struggle nor pure parliamentary politics could be construed by some as ideologically adulterated, or a 'sell out'. In fact, what McKearney and others proposed was a tactic that could prove highly effective in instigating powerful social change, the tactic of 'mass protest', which could utilise parliamentary politics and even armed struggle as part of its weaponry yet was broad enough to overcome the limitations inherent in both. McKearney remembers:

My view at that time was, I suppose, a sort of syndicalist view. Some of us thought that we should create a mass movement outside the parliamentary system. It would include organised Labour, H-block protest supporters and other interest groups. The blanket protest had some support among ordinary working people in the south. This was pre-'Celtic Tiger' days, with unemployment of fifteen to twenty per cent. Ireland was losing tens of thousands of its young people every year through emigration. Mass protest was known at the time. In 1979, for example, there was a mass protest of about 200,000 people, against the high levels of income tax at the time. The protesters were a mixture of workers, bourgeois and anybody really who was affected by the tax situation. It was a bit like the [later] British Poll Tax demonstrations, in that it was broad collection of interests. So some of us thought there'd be an opportunity to broaden the struggle with these various other interest groups.

A mass movement could be energised, it could make demands without being curbed by the compromises necessary in parliamentary politics. Of course there could be a role for parliamentary politics, but my view was that it shouldn't be the be-all and end-all. At that time, I thought we could become a vehicle for progressive politics. We could have given such a movement structure, confidence and direction.

Around that time I thought we had been boxed in by our opponents. We had been confined to the Republican constituency in the north and I thought we could reach out more. The southern state had us boxed in. Diplomatically, the British had us boxed in and undermined us internationally at every opportunity. Armed struggle was a tactic that had to actually deliver something. It was valid while delivering results was a possibility. Armed struggle is a means to an end. It's not what it is all about in itself. So if it's ever not delivering, then you simply have to stop. You have to stop putting your own people through all of that, through the torture of it all. I also thought that we needed much more of a southern support base.

My problem with electoral politics is that they are at best reformist – never revolutionary. Big capital controls everything. So what can you really achieve? And you'd have to spend so much time and energy jumping through hoop after hoop. And you'd be doing all that just to go from maybe one representative to two representatives, or maybe from two to four, and so on.

So there was a re-evaluation going on well before the hunger strikes. I think the hunger strikes propelled us down a particular route. But the build up of that re-evaluation process was going to show up somewhere. If it hadn't have been the hunger strikes, it would have been something else, maybe something less dramatic, but it would have come through and some other sort of political activity working alongside armed struggle would inevitably have resulted.

MacStiofian [Provisional IRA Chief Of Staff from 1969 to 1973] of course had gone on hunger strike in 1973. He had made these bellicose statements, like "either I'll be dead or free". And four IRA men were caught trying to rescue him. They got long sentences. As to the story being that the Army Council ordered him off his strike, that is true but it seems he had actually ended it himself some time previously by taking some sort of sustenance. It was announced that he'd taken, I don't know, milk or something. We thought, no way, that's just propaganda. A lot of volunteers had invested a lot of faith in him and so were reluctant to believe that he'd broken his strike. But it soon became clear that he was definitely taking something. He'd effectively broken his strike. And it all became a bit embarrassing. So I think that's when the Army Council ordered him to come off the strike. It was really just formalising the actual situation. He did lose face for not seeing it through. I didn't think he was bad oul' devil, you know. But he'd made such a show of it all, with his comments at the beginning and not seeing it through, it sort of finished his Republican career.

While the option of a serious, mass hunger strike was being considered in 1980, the movement had to contend with the prospect of potentially differing perspectives between those engaged in activism or other activities on the outside and the IRA members inside the H-blocks. – although that fear appeared not have become realised in that way. McKearney recalls:

Things inevitably were different on the inside, in jail. But I don't think you could say that there was an inside/outside split of opinion. There were as many differences of opinion inside the jail as outside. And maybe inside you'd be more reflective, in a sense, for obvious reasons. And, of course, being on the inside did have some impact on the way you saw things. For instance we were not just ordinary prisoners – we were IRA men in jail. There was an intensity of this shared experience.

And you could say that, on the outside, day-to-day life was diluted by non-IRA things. On the inside, it was pretty much all IRA things. So that had it's own intensity. And we had no access to literature, and so on. The only book we had was the Bible. I read the Bible twice, which I, an atheist, take great delight in telling some Christians.

Another factor is that in prison you tended to get particular types of prisoners. Now this is a broad generalisation. But the IRA men in jail tended to be those who'd be at the front of things. You could say that generally the most adventurous, the most idealistic, the most committed, the most dogmatic and the most passionate volunteers would either end up dead or in jail. There'd be others who learned to survive by avoiding conflict. Some who'd be more attuned to the compromises needed for local realities. Some would need to be like that in order to direct operations, and so on. And as I say, it is a general point. It wouldn't be true to say everyone who avoided jail was never in the front line. But the ones who ended up in jail tended not to be the ones that cried off jobs with like, the baby's not well or the wife's sick, or whatever. There's a thing called "Four o'clock courage", like there'd be a lot waiting to get involved in particular operations the night before, but come 4 o'clock, they'd be a lot thinner on the ground. Like I say, a generalisation. And maybe you'd have some in jail that didn't really cause an awful lot of damage. There's a saying that you can get crazy pilots and you can get old pilots, but you don't get many crazy old pilots.

So there was an intensity, a concentration, a focus in the jail, which mundane matters outside couldn't impact on. But there was still as big a variety of views inside as there was outside. In fact, I was speaking to an old friend recently and we said, you know, if we were twenty-five instead of forty-five when the Good Friday Agreement came around, would we have voted for it?

By the time the first hunger strike was under way, the British were desperate to uncover what the prisoners were thinking, the state of their morale and what they might accept as a settlement at particular points. The prisoners were, of course, alive to attempts to spy on them. McKearney agreed with the suggestion that the British used spies and infiltration in an attempt to stay one step ahead of the escalating protests. He recalls:

We'd speak in Irish, which was good for baffling the "big boots", the screws in the Blocks. But I'm sure all the Brits had to do was tape record us and take it away and get it translated, which I was sure they could do. The security level in the IRA was pretty good but I think it is a credible assumption that there was a relatively highly placed informer in the Belfast Brigade. And some of the H-block Committees, sure, you could walk into some of these.

I remember one time ... Cardinal Tomás Ó Fiaich [Catholic Primate of Ireland whose aim was to bring an end to the prison protests] and Edward Daly [Catholic Bishop of Derry] visited Thatcher and she tells them of a proposal related to clothing, that the prisoners don't have to wear uniforms. This was on a Thursday – Cabinet day is a Thursday. Now, the hunger strike was to start on Monday. It was announced on the news that clothing was being conceded. The Board Of Visitors (BOV) came to our wing and a woman whom I had not seen with the BOV before met with Brendan Hughes, the OC. She asked him if this concession on clothing would be enough to avert the strike. He said: "No, we have five demands." An hour or two later, after this visit, the British issued a statement "clarifying" the British offer, saying that it had been "civilian-type" clothing that had been on offer. This was not what Cardinal Ó Fiaich understood from his meeting with Thatcher at all. All of which makes you doubt it was a serious offer.

The duplicity of the British in failing to make "a serious offer" to the hunger strikers in 1980 is seen by historian and author Tim Pat Coogan as a grave error – one that essentially guaranteed another hunger strike whose participants would take their protest all the way. The result would be a propaganda disaster for the British akin to the firing squads of 1916. Coogan recalls his experience in the winter of 1980:

Charlie Haughey called on me, seeing me as an "insider". His adviser was Padriag O'hAnnrachain. I was advising him, and he was advising Haughey. I advised them on heading off the hunger strike and then on ending it once it had started. Then the British and the prisoners seemed to have a deal and the strike ended. Sean McKenna was in a bad way and the British played on that.

A few days later, on Christmas day in fact, Fr Brendan Meagher [the priest who reportedly acted as a go-between for the British government and the prisoners] came to see me at home. He said that the prisoners

felt conned. They'd understood that the deal meant that they'd be allowed to wear their own clothes and, in fact, their relatives had brought
them clothes up to the jail. But the prisoners had not received them and
now there were bad vibes coming out the place. I wrote at the time in
the *Irish Press* that things did not look good at all. The prisoners were
being messed about. And the warders, mostly drawn from the Loyalist
community, were giving them stick. We knew that we had to get
things sorted out quickly or a new hunger strike would start very soon
– and this time it would certainly be to the death.

I spoke to Michael Allison, Northern Ireland Prison Minister, saying a settlement was in everyone's interest, and that the hunger strikers could make 1916 look like a picnic. He actually agreed but said:
"Remember, there is a lady in the case." Thatcher had, in my view,
decided from day one that she would take it all the way. I know they
drafted in some Donegal Gaelic speakers to work out what the prisoners were saying in Irish. And she was determined to pursue the policy
of criminalisation.

Another hunger striker who remembers this period well is Laurence
McKeown. He was born in Randalstown, Co Antrim, and was arrested in
August 1976 for suspected IRA activities. In April 1977, he was sentenced
to life imprisonment. McKeown spent the next four-and-a-half years on
the blanket and then, from 1978, the no-wash protest in the H-blocks. In a
reflection of how steep a mountain the protesters had to climb in terms of
generating public support at that time, according to McKeown a then RTE
reporter Mary McAleese – now the president of the Republic of Ireland
– was told by her superiors in RTE that the H-block protests story was "of
no interest".

In October 1980, McKeown volunteered to hunger strike but never took
part, as that strike was over before he was called – the prisoners believing
that the British government was going to satisfy the demand for political
status. When a second hunger strike was called for March 1981, McKeown
again volunteered and went on his strike on June 29. He fasted for seventy
days before his family intervened to authorise medical attention. Released
from Long Kesh in 1992, he sheds further light on the feeling among
Republicans that during the first hunger strike of 1980 the British authorities had no intention of making a genuine attempt to reach a compromise.
He recalls:

It was said by the British [to Cardinal Ó Fiaich and others] that once the strike was ended, there would be concessions on at least the wearing of our own clothes, as opposed to prison uniform. Ó Fiaich had appealed to the hunger strikers and to the British government to call off the strike. He thought he had an understanding that our own clothes would be acceptable. And this was the understanding of Republicans at the time. So our relatives brought our own clothes up to the prison to leave in for us to wear, thinking that that was what had been agreed. But instead we were told that we couldn't wear them, and that we would have to wear "prison-issue civilian clothing", which was not what had been agreed at all.

Many years later, during the making of a documentary on Ireland by the BBC, the BBC producer said off-screen that he'd been told by someone who'd been in official circles at the time that six NIO officials including the prison governor had threatened to resign if the prisoners had been given any concessions at all.

Despite setbacks, strong morale and ingenuity drove forward the mass politicisation of the prison protest in 1980-1 as the struggle in the cells engaged the sympathies and grievances of the wider Nationalist community. It nevertheless remained a risky strategy. McKeown reveals more about the reservations that some in the IRA, both on the inside and the outside had about the IRA being seen to weaken its military stance. This was set against the views of those, (including some blanketmen) who saw the value of votes that were there for the taking. Certainly, the reservations became more subdued after Sands's crucial victory.

There was a river of communication flowing as we had comms, relative's visits, comrades' visits, newspaper cuttings – we even had radios smuggled in. So we were able to sense that something was happening on the outside. It might not have been happening at the pace we felt it should but something was being done on our behalf on the outside that seemed to be making some headway.

[However] the leadership outside the prisons [had] thought that hunger striking would be a distraction. The option had been discussed since POW status had been withdrawn in March 1976. We had been advised to try a different approach. But by now [1980] we'd tried various protests and were no closer to resolving the issue.

Among the Blanketmen were some of the most irreverent Republicans you could get. While some were from established Republican families, many were not. Many would have joined the IRA in the early and mid-70s, as a reaction to the Troubles at that time. And many would have had no Republican background, and so maybe wouldn't have had the same hang ups about electoral politics as the maybe more traditional Republicans might have had. Some of the more traditional Republican types might have been a bit more conservative, Catholic, and steeped in the history and values of Republicanism. Whereas many of the newer Republicans would have looked at the IRSP and Irish Independent Party winning votes in local elections in 1981 during the hunger strike and been saying: "That's votes we should have had. Why are they running and getting our votes?"

The debate at that point would have been about involvement in electoral politics whilst still retaining an abstentionist position regarding Dail Eireann and Westminster. It was [not until] years later, once the impact of engagement in electoral politics had been evidenced that the issue of abstentionism from Dail Eireann came up. And then came Frank Maguire's death. You know, if it had been any other seat, we would have most likely lost. Frank was an old-time Republican, from the 1950s campaign, whose support for the prisoners was clear. He'd visit us, bring us tobacco and stuff like that. So when he unfortunately died, many thought, we could win this seat. There had always been a strong Republican tradition in the area. There were still debates about fighting elections but when Bobby won, well, who could argue with that? From then on the focus of the movement changed

It was a big risk though. We had nothing to base any expectations on. It's not like now when you can look back, say, three years and say well, last time he got this per cent or this many votes. At that time, there was absolutely no history to go on. We really didn't know if he'd win. It was about gaining support and putting on a good campaign. We'd get lots of information on how it was going. We had to be on our guard when relatives or supporters were telling us during visits how well it was going, in case they were just trying to keep your spirits up. But as things went on we realised there was a chance. Of course some in the movement had done their homework and so I think they would have been a bit more confident than some [others]. But, as I say, there was no history. There were still debates and all after that, but a step had been taken.

McKeown suggests that behind the Thatcher government's iron determination to break the prisoners, the apparent inability of the British to
comprehend the appeal the hunger strike struggle had to the historic sense
of oppression and injustice in the Nationalist psyche may have proved a
hidden trump card when it came to Sands's election. Certainly, failure to
reckon with the vitality of the issues at stake damaged the image of the
Catholic Church in some Republican eyes, an institution with the potential
to be a powerful local and international support network yet one which
failed to back the protest.

> You know, the final irony of the whole tragedy is that in setting out to
> criminalize us, the British legitimised and politicised us in ways that
> no-one could have foreseen at the time. It was like they hadn't ever
> read a history book. I mean, Thatcher apparently said to one of her aids,
> after I think seven men were dead, "Is it some macho thing?" I mean,
> they hadn't a clue. It was a colonial mentality that had prevailed. I can't
> remember who said it, but there is a quote that says: "The colonised
> have to understand the coloniser – but the coloniser does not need to
> understand the colonised".
>
> At the time the protests and then the hunger strikes changed many
> things on the ground. For instance I know people, older people, who
> were devout Catholics, who have not been back to mass since. The
> perception of the Church, especially among working-class Catholics,
> and even established rural Republican families, was that the Church
> not only couldn't do anything to help, but in the end didn't want to do
> anything to help. It saw the groundswell of Republican feeling spread-
> ing through the Nationalist community and it was like it was competi-
> tion to them. I'm sure it was partly a hierarchy thing, and many priests
> would have not seen it like that – but many did. The whole thing about
> not letting Republicans have the national flag on their coffins was just
> a joke. When British soldiers died and were buried in their country they
> had the Union Jack on their coffin, so why not Republicans? In the
> end, the Church just wanted it to be over. In the end, the Church just
> wanted it to end, even if it meant defeat and criminalisation.

Another major Irish institution that Republican hunger strikers and activists felt betrayed by was Charles Haughey's Fianna Fail government in
the south. McKeown reflects on the learning process that made he and his

comrades come to realise what they were up against in taking on the British state's sweeping cultural and political hegemony, which not only cowed the Church, but also reached over the border into the supposedly independent Republic.

> Some of us were really naive. We had this feeling in the beginning, "Oh you know, Charlie Haughey and all that, they'll do something". After all, Fianna Fail considered themselves to have the Republican mantle. Fianna Fail calls itself "The Republican Party". But he gave Thatcher a silver teapot. We eventually wised up and realised that they felt threatened, too. Maybe Nationalists now had an option they did not have before and it was a revolutionary Republican one. Dublin had sat on their hands for so long. In many ways, it was too late for them. We felt let down, too, because when anyone abroad, like the USA for example, would press the Brits, they could always say: "Well, we're just doing what the Irish government is doing … " which was nothing. How could other governments argue with that?

Chapter Nine:

Tricks and traps

From the British perspective, to defeat the hunger strikers at this juncture, in 1980, was an especially attractive proposition. They'd guessed it would be a bloody battle but were prepared to see it through at all costs. To back down would concede the legitimacy of the Republican (and Loyalist) right to arms. This, the British authorities realised, would represent an enormous propaganda victory for the IRA and so they sought to use every means at their disposal to win the battle of the H-blocks.

Nationalists, concerned about prisoners' conditions in the late 1970s as they protested against the withdrawal of Special Category Status and went first "on the blanket" and then on the "no-wash" protest, were initially confounded by the lack of will on the part of the British to avoid the hunger strike many felt was inexorably approaching. It was, after all, the next logical step. And yet the British were, in fact, only too willing to take on the IRA in the battlefield of the prisons.

Many prison staff considered the threat of hunger strike to be a bluff, a tactic to get more concessions. Whether genuine or not, many in the British Army, intelligence community and Cabinet — not least Thatcher herself, believed this was a battle they couldn't lose. Men would die, the IRA would be demoralised and, once and for all, the opportunity to defeat them would present itself. Of course, they would like to defeat the IRA without the public relation concerns that hunger strikes inevitably would raise. But they believed the storm could be coped with.

What the British did not foresee, however, was that the showdown would result in the radicalisation of a dormant Republican electoral base, and the politicisation of many ordinary Nationalists. In other words, in the British misreading of Irish history, and therefore the current situation, they did not realise that the traditional abstainers and reluctant SDLP voters could conceivably join forces with the H-block campaigners and effectively create a "new" grouping – and an uncompromisingly revolutionary one at that.

The British had also gotten used to the idea that they had the IRA on the run. While some undoubtedly thought this was simply prudent propaganda to dish out, many in senior positions, especially in the intelligence agencies, considered that the IRA had been on the defensive since 1974, perhaps even earlier. They were looking for the elusive knockout blow they were convinced they could deliver – if only the government would let them take the gloves off. Certainly this view was revised somewhat in 1979, but not by all. For some, the conviction that the IRA were still on the ropes, as many around 1975/76 had believed they were – including some in the IRA – was not given up until after the hunger strikes. This led some to eagerly look forward to what they imagined would be the IRA's last stand. Indeed in May 1981, with the second hunger strike well under way, Thatcher confidently declared the hunger strikes the IRA's "last card".

From 1979 until September 1981, the incoming Thatcher government was represented in the Six Counties/Northern Ireland by Humphrey Atkins, Thatcher's Secretary of State for Northern Ireland. From his days running the NIO, he is remembered as an extremely tough man, who knew his own mind, who was bright, funny and could (on appropriate occasions) hold an impressive amount of liquor. A former Royal Navy man, he is remembered with affection and respect by many people he came into contact with.

"Jim" worked closely with Atkins as a junior minister during his time in Thatcher's Cabinet. Living in England and now somewhat elderly, Jim offers insights into the thinking of Atkins and the government as they faced the hunger strikers, as well as more general reminiscences on Atkins's character which clearly underline Jim's enduring respect.

Atkins, in Jim's view, was totally loyal to Thatcher and her policies. If instructed to take a specific course of action, Atkins followed the line implicitly and without deviation. Jim contends this was particularly evident during the 1980 hunger strike. The same could not be said, according to Jim, of fellow NIO Minister Michael Allison.

Atkins, in Jim's recollection, initially thought the hunger strike was a token gesture by Republicans at the Maze/Long Kesh. Intelligence, as indicated by other contributors from the security services, was surprisingly poor in this regard. Surprising in the sense of, with a supposed informer relatively well placed in the Belfast Brigade of the IRA at the time, they ought to have realised the strength of feeling the prisoners had after years of struggle and guessed that they were serious. These prisoners were men who had, after all, worn nothing but a blanket for more than three years and lived in their own filth for two. They were clearly not playing at it.

Despite this knowledge, which you did not need to be superspy to come across (a glance at An Phoblacht would have done the trick), there was a stated belief that it would last no more than a few weeks – during which time it would gain insufficient momentum to sustain it or make it a major political issue. Jim says this belief was based entirely on assessments supplied to the government by the intelligence services. Atkins was a clever fellow but at the end of the day, a minister is guided by intelligence. It was only as time went on that it became clear to Atkins that Republicans were intent on seeing the strike through to its ultimate conclusion. A suggestion has also been made from a different source that Atkins saw only the intelligence some wanted him to see and no more. Furthermore, it has been mooted that perhaps his superior knew more than she let on.

While Atkins was undoubtedly loyal to Thatcher, according to Jim and others he was considered by some of her entourage to be a "Wet" – meaning someone with an instinct to dilute or soften the Thatcher message, or even a conservative who would fundamentally disagree with Thatcher policy. Being cast as a Wet was political death under Thatcher.

Within the first week of the hunger strike, the intelligence services began reporting that Republicans had deliberately timed the strike to reach its peak during the 1980 Christmas period. The strategy seemed logical to Atkins and his team: the death of a hunger striker then would be much more emotive, provoking a greater reaction at what is universally seen as a family time.

Jim claims the intelligence services had a mole inside the Republican movement at the Maze/Long Kesh. This individual, he claimed, was a "highly placed and respected Republican" who kept the intelligence services regularly updated on the thinking and political direction of the prisoners. Now, bearing in mind how intelligence appeared to underestimated Republican resolve at the beginning of the 1980 strike, one has to conclude, that either the source was not telling all he knew, or that he was not very good. Of course, it could be that there really was no source, though for someone like Jim to mention it after so many years makes that scenario improbable. Perhaps the source was not as highly placed as Jim would like to believe.

Jim claims the government knew that decisions relating to the strike were taken by Brendan Hughes and the six other hunger strikers in conjunction with the OCs of all the Republican H-blocks. It should be pointed out, however, that this is now known from the many publications that have appeared on the subject since. Jim also claims that these meetings were continually monitored by the intelligence services and the Maze/Long Kesh authorities. But if this were indeed the case, it still leaves the obvious gaps in the British reading of the situation at the time unexplained. Jim did not say how these meetings were monitored, so we don't know the efficiency of the methods involved.

As soon as it became clear what the long-term Republican objective was – nothing less than the five demands and full political status – Jim recalls that Thatcher decided upon her policy of no compromise. If we are to believe some other intelligence sources for this book, however, Thatcher's policy had been decided previously when her initial briefings told her – Mountbatten and Warrenpoint notwithstanding – that the IRA was beatable since it was at a point where it was unsure of both its support levels and future direction.

This view would also suggest that the notion of IRA prisoners hunger striking to the death (and ultimately to defeat) did not appal hawkish British minds. If a wise owl in the administration had investigated the likely courses of action open to the protesting prisoners in the H-blocks in 1979, they would have concluded that hunger striking was actually the most likely assuming no concessions were made in relation to the blanket and no-wash protests. In fact, one source has gone further, suggesting maybe it was no accident that the treatment meted out to the prisoners actually increased their resolve to select the hunger striking option. Was it really then, so this view continues, such a surprise that a hunger strike took place?

Such claims should be treated with caution. Nonetheless, it is reasonably clear that everyone from the Relatives Action Committees and Sinn Fein to other Nationalist politicians and the Church were pointing to the rapidly materialising spectre of hunger strike. Is it credible, therefore, to believe that the only people who did not see it coming were the British government? Of course, they could have seen it coming and not really understood the challenge by which they about to be confronted. But the post-Warrenpoint Army and post-Airey Neave Thatcher (Neave, Thatcher's security guru, was assassinated by the INLA just before Thatcher came to power in 1979) were uniquely focused on defeating the IRA. It is not beyond reason that if they did not provoke the crisis, then at least they were not unwelcoming of the opportunity to take on the IRA through the prisoners.

Given Thatcher's future modus operandi while reconstructing (some would say deconstructing) British industrial life in the 1980s, it is worth considering claims that her government generally provoked her enemies at a time of her choosing: steel workers in 1980 and mineworkers in 1984, for example. These were both lengthy crises that appeared at first glance to have fallen upon the Thatcher government, and certainly others played a part in bringing them to a head. Yet subsequent investigations have found clear evidence that both had been meticulously prepared for.

Consider a report by one of Thatcher's key aides, Nicholas Ridley, in relation to the mining industry. Written in 1978, six years before the miners' strike, the Ridley Report stated that in order to carry through Thatcherite reform of that industry, the National Union Of Mineworkers would need to be confronted at a time of the government's choosing and defeated as an effective union. Preparations for this strike would include importing coal to ensure stocks were high, thus minimising the effect of no coal production during the strike. In the event, the pit selected by the government to provoke the miners was Corttonwood in the heart of South Yorkshire, home of NUM leader Arthur Scargill, and the headquarters of the NUM. This decision would take the battle to the "enemy within", as Thatcher called the miners' union. Elaborate plans were drawn up for mobile police units that would combat pickets who would try to ensure a complete closedown of the industry during the strike. Many other plans are detailed in Seumas Milne's classic account, *The Enemy Within* (not to be confused with Martin Dillon's book of the same name dealing with the IRA in England). Suffice to say here that if the Thatcherites went to such elaborate lengths to defeat an unarmed opponent of the regime, it is conceivable that the they took at least the same care in relation to plans regarding the IRA

During their last two years in opposition, bearing in mind the weakness of the Callaghan Labour government, the Thatcherites were effectively an administration in waiting. Thatcher's future opponents were well known to her and her supporters. Plans were drawn up to deal with "enemies of the future Conservative government". That did not guarantee their effective implementation, of course, but it did demonstrate strategic thinking. Given such careful preparation, how surprised could Thatcher be that hunger striking would be the result of a campaign to humiliate Republican prisoners?

In 1980, the "no compromise" instruction regarding the IRA prison protests was passed to the NIO and to Atkins in person. Jim is adamant that Atkins was told directly by Thatcher not to consider granting or acceding to any of the demands on which the hunger strike was based. Atkins was told not to countenance any form of face-to-face negotiations to resolve the crisis within the Maze/Long Kesh, as this would legitimise the prisoners. Jim recalls Atkins commenting that, in line with this official policy, he was not prepared to speak with people whose only axe to grind was political status, that being off the agenda as far as the British were concerned.

However, this official line was not followed by all members of the NIO team during the first hunger strike of 1980. Jim claims the NIO Prisons Minister, Michael Allison, was more willing to negotiate with the prisoners. He claims that Allison viewed the strike as a protest over prison conditions and not as a battle to obtain special status. Allison was not unintelligent either, and was not blind to the prisoners' drive to political status of some sort. But he was of the view that the IRA's real objective could be contained by dealing with the prison conditions issue at face value. The Authorities would not need to grant all five demands, and so could not be said to have granted political status. By appearing flexible, and perhaps even conceding one or two of the demands, then the authorities, so went this view, would have wrong-footed the IRA and defused what was sure to be a crisis of sorts. Allison's attitude was known to the intelligence services and was a matter of some concern within the NIO team – especially to Atkins who saw him as a potential weak link in the solid official stance at that time. Atkins also feared Allison's attitude could undermine the NIO should it ever become public knowledge.

Jim relates that it appeared to him as though Allison was prepared to end the strike by reasoning with the prisoners. Comments made by the Prisons Minister during early December 1980 apparently revealed he had hinted to the prisoners that their campaign against the government was useless as they would be unable to concede to the demands. To do so would be to hand the Maze/Long Kesh over to the prisoners and turn it into nothing more than a holiday camp. Jim recalls he felt at the time that Allison was trying to prepare the ground for discussions with strike leader Brendan Hughes.

Out of these alleged discussions arises the matter of the "document", allegedly given to the protesting prisoners by the British government. This is the document referred to in Beresford's *Ten Men Dead*, of which was said by an IRA Army Council member at the time: "It's full of holes, you could drive a bus through it". The document had been dramatically flown to Aldergrove Airport in the company of an MI6 officer liaising with the Republican movement and codenamed "The Mountain Climber". It was given to a Priest, codenamed "The Angel", to take to IRA leaders in a safe house in west Belfast. The document appeared to hold out the bare minimum of hope that some concessions on clothing, at least, might be achievable – but only after the hunger strike had been called off. At this stage, one of the seven men on hunger strike, Sean McKenna, was hours from death after 53 days without food. The leader of the hunger strike, Brendan Hughes, also on hunger strike, was faced with the choice: negotiate while McKenna will probably die, reject the document, which would presumably sentence McKenna to death, or accept and save McKenna's life, and still negotiate on the basis of the document. He chose to accept the document and save McKenna's life.

However, as we have seen, when the IRA in the jail attempted to implement the agreement they thought they had in the document, after they had called off the first hunger strike after 53 days, the prison governor and the British stalled. Eventually the agreement on clothes turned out to be either misinterpreted or non-existent, depending whose version you believed. Either way, it appeared that the British had behaved in bad faith simply to have the hunger strike called off and the prisoners defeated. If that is true, then clearly there was no real attempt to negotiate at all. The IRA could have meekly accepted defeat or, alternatively, realised they had been duped on this occasion and immediately plan another hunger strike. When asked whether, in fact, the document was designed to trick the Republican hunger strikers off their fast, Jim unhesitatingly and emphatically replies: "Yes!"

Jim insists the IRA prisoners were given an advance copy of a statement Atkins was due to make in the House of Commons regarding the situation at the prison. He claims the document was delivered into the prison but refuses to identify the individual who delivered it. The document was called *Regimes in Northern Ireland's Prisons: Prisoners' day-to-day life with special emphasis on the Maze and Armagh*. Jim provides the following details from his notebooks of the time:

> 5th December 1980 – National H Block Committee asked for a personal meeting with HA [Humphrey Atkins] – request refused.
> 8th December 1980 – Thatcher, Carrington, Atkins and Geoffrey Howe met with the Taoiseach and senior Irish officials in Dublin re the hunger strike.
> 12th December 1980 – UDA prisoners began a hunger strike at the Maze [The strike lasts just 5 days ending on 17th December].

15th December 1980 – IRA hunger striker Sean McKenna moved to
Musgrave Park hospital after serious concern at his deteriorating condition. NIO decision in conjunction with Downing Street.

17th December 1980 – Catholic Cardinal Tomás Ó Fiaich called for an
end to the hunger strike. Ó Fiaich called upon Thatcher to personally
intervene.

18th December 1980 – IRA hunger strike called off.

In Jim's informed view, he claims the strike was called off after the prisoners were successfully misled into thinking their demands would be met.
Because McKenna was close to death, there was a view the prisoners would
be "receptive" to a proposed settlement that came near their demands.
However, Jim recalls he personally believed nothing was to be conceded in
actuality at any time.

Jim looks back on the denial Atkins made of any last-minute deal or
document as being particularly disappointing. He felt Atkins had been put
in a position where he had to deny this had happened. Jim believed the
intelligence services, whom he maintains had far too much influence inside
the Thatcher administration, had insisted on this approach. Jim stresses the
prisoners did get an advance copy of the Atkins statement to parliament.

He points out that the intelligence services, especially MI6, were an invis-
ible yet ever-present force within the NIO during November and December
1980. He describes them as a "cancer which quickly invaded the body politic
that was the NIO in 1980". He also maintains the second hunger strike
could have been averted had the NIO followed up the December 1980
document.

The relationship between Atkins and Thatcher, Jim recalls, was never the
same following the events of late 1980. Atkins felt he was carrying blame for
events over which he never had full control. The decision to move Atkins
from Secretary of State in September 1981 and make him Deputy Foreign
Secretary came, in Jim's recollection, as a complete body blow. Atkins re-
sented the move and his resentment voiced itself in public criticism of the
government's handling of the Falklands crisis of 1982. As a result of this
criticism Atkins was forced to resign.

Jim's remarks raise the question as to who was really running the government side during the run-up and in 1980. Was it the NIO or the intelligence community? "Oliver" is a former member of the intelligence services.
During his period of service he completed three tours of duty in Northern

Ireland experiencing first hand the web of intrigue and deceit that was, and still is, an ever-present ingredient of the "dirty war".

Oliver arrived in Northern Ireland for his second tour of duty as in intelligence operative in mid-1980, shortly before the prison issue finally came to a head. He recalls how one of his primary functions was to glean as much information as possible on the developing tensions within the Republican movement over who had real control of the prison issue.

By the autumn of 1980, recalls Oliver, the intelligence services knew opinion within the H-blocks favoured the option of a hunger strike as the weapon to finally deliver the Republican prisoners' demands. However, it was also known that the IRA leadership did not welcome the possibility of a hunger strike, believing it created an emotional focus that would have a detrimental impact on the ongoing military campaign. The IRA leadership also recognised the potential of an adverse effect should the hunger-strike "weapon" fail. However, despite attempting to control and manage the prisons issue, the IRA leadership appeared not to have correctly gauged the depth of feeling inside the Maze/Long Kesh.

Oliver reveals that it soon became clear to the intelligence services that a hunger strike was the only thing that would resolve the crisis within the Republican movement – one way or the other. It was known that emerging figures within the Republican leadership, such as Gerry Adams, opposed the idea of a hunger strike. Oliver explains:

> We were aware of IRA concerns about a hunger strike. Some of the leaders had major concerns, not least because of the possibility of failure. There is an old IRA belief: "Break the lads in prison and you break the lads outside." Furthermore, Republicans were only too well aware that a defeat in the Maze prison could also affect levels of support on the outside. That, I believe is the real reason why the IRA tried to prevent the first hunger strike getting off the ground. However, the IRA leadership could not ignore the strength of the prison population, and it eventually agreed to back the 1980 hunger strike which began in late October.

Oliver maintains the British government was briefed and made fully conversant with the intelligence situation leading up to the first hunger strike in 1980. He has little doubt that it was "allowed to go ahead".

In my opinion, and I stress it is my opinion, there was a belief within the Thatcher administration that the hunger strike could prove to be a means to damage the IRA in the long term. Intelligence showed the divisions within the IRA over the tactic. Failure, I think, the government believed would seriously damage IRA support. Therefore it was imperative that the hard-line approach be adopted and maintained – no concessions to IRA prisoners' demands'.

Oliver believes thinking behind the scenes generally reflected Thatcher's public position on the hunger strike in November 1980, when she said publicly: "Let me make one point about the hunger strike in the Maze prison. I want this to be utterly clear. There can be no political justification for murder or any other crime. The government will never concede political status to the hunger strikers, or to any others convicted of criminal offences in the Province."

Oliver describes the period of the first hunger strike as one of "intensity". It was a time of highly secret negotiations involving the British and Irish governments. There was, he said, evidence of real concern of possible destabilisation within the Haughey administration in Dublin should a hunger striker die. Tensions were further heightened when three women prisoners at Armagh jail and a further 23 men at the Maze/Long Kesh joined the hunger strike in December. However, Oliver claims the intelligence services knew the situation at the Maze/Long Kesh could have been defused and resolved by a single concession.

We knew by early December 1980 that the IRA wanted a face-saving solution to the hunger strike. Our sources were telling us had the IRA prisoners been allowed to wear tracksuits and trainers – a kind of tacit recognition that they did not have the "criminal" status – the strike would have ended. That information went up the line, but no concessions were forthcoming. But what eventually did happen simply paved the way for the 1981 hunger strike in which 10 IRA men died.

Oliver believes the British government duped the IRA into believing the prisoners' demands had been granted. He said the British government deliberately created a state of confusion among the hunger strikers by moving McKenna, who was close to death, to a hospital outside the prison. He said this had the effect of creating uncertainty within his colleagues, who would not know if he was about to die or had in fact died. At the same time, the government also let it be known that a document from the Foreign Office in London was on its way to the prison via a trusted priest – Oliver thinks this was Fr Brendan Meagher. The document was handed over to the priest at a supposedly secret meeting at Belfast's Aldergrove airport by MI6 officer Michael Oatley, a.k.a. "the Mountain Climber".

In fact, claims Oliver, the Aldergrove meeting took place in view of RUC Special Branch personnel. He confirms that the document was seen by members of the IRA leadership at a safe house in Belfast before it was handed over to prisoners at the Maze/Long Kesh. They were far from happy with what they read. News of the document's imminent arrival created a dilemma for the prisoners, something Oliver now believes was a deliberate tactic by the British. The prisoners' OC, Hughes, was faced with the problem previously related, i.e., did he allow McKenna to die for concessions that had already been agreed? And, as we have seen, Hughes called off the hunger strike without waiting for the document to arrive. Oliver believes that the British had actually scored a senseless pyrrhic victory, since the prisoners, realising they had been conned, immediately toughened their resolve and began preparing for another strike.

> Initially, the British government thought they had won; the strike was over, the IRA defeated. In reality all they had succeeded in doing was setting the stage for the hunger strike of 1981. Oatley and the Foreign Office had succeeded in ending the strike, but I now firmly believe the British authorities deliberately and carefully constructed this document with no other purpose in mind but to con the IRA into thinking they were getting the concessions they were demanding. MI6, I believe, deliberately orchestrated and manipulated this situation for their own purposes. We were all kept in the dark about what was really going on. Even the Irish government was misled by the British over many things at that point in time. However, the question has to be asked just whose purposes were ultimately served - certainly not the countless British soldiers, RUC officers or civilians who lost their lives in a further decade of violence.

The Foreign Office document had been extremely vague and mentioned the possibility of some movement once the strike had ended. There was initial confusion within the IRA ranks about what had or had not been granted in relation to the prisoner's demands. It soon became obvious to the IRA that the prisoner's efforts had produced absolutely nothing. Oliver again:

> Within a short time our sources were telling us IRA prisoners were again gearing up for another hunger strike. This time it would be led by Bobby Sands who had taken over as IRA OC in the Maze prison. We also knew that, once again, the IRA leadership opposed the move and had made it clear the military campaign would not be suspended if the strike took place.
>
> Despite this position, we knew the IRA leadership recognised that a second hunger strike was on the cards and that they would have to bow to the inevitable. Personally, I have no doubt that the second hunger strike and the deaths of ten men could and should have been prevented. By literally duping IRA prisoners into ending the 1980 strike the British government only succeeded in deepening the mistrust and animosity that already existed inside the Maze prison.

The second IRA hunger strike began on March 1, 1981, the fifth anniversary of the ending of Special Category Status. But the strike was quickly overtaken by other events – the death of Fermanagh-South Tyrone Independent MP Frank Maguire.

Oliver reveals that intelligence reports indicated individuals within the Republican movement were in favour of an IRA prisoner contesting the Fermanagh-South Tyrone by-election. But the reports also indicated senior Republicans had concerns that if a hunger striker were chosen and not elected, then it could be interpreted as being poor support for the strike or the prisoners' cause. Sinn Fein called a meeting in Monaghan to weigh up the risks of running a candidate. The reports also showed there were differing opinions within Sinn Fein about whether or not their candidate should have a "clear run" against any Unionist opponent. As it transpired, the idea of running a Sinn Fein prisoner as a candidate was rejected when it was first put to Sinn Fein delegates attending the meeting.

However, people such as former Sinn Fein Director of Publicity Danny Morrison favoured Sands's candidacy, realising it was the perfect opportunity to gain publicity for the hunger strike. Reports also showed the idea of a hunger-strike candidate was supported by other senior IRA activists. When the idea was put to Sinn Fein delegates a second time, it was passed and Sands was chosen to contest the Fermanagh-South Tyrone seat. Oliver claims the Thatcher administration was made aware of the threat, but failed to respond appropriately.

> At that stage alarm bells should have been ringing within the British government. Our reports to them made it clear strength and support for Bobby Sands was growing and there was a very real possibility an H-block prisoner/hunger striker would take the Fermanagh-South Tyrone seat at Westminster. It appears those warnings fell upon deaf ears, or upon the ears of those individuals who had a different strategy in mind. Anyway, Sands was duly elected MP for Fermanagh-South Tyrone on 9th April 1981 when he defeated Ulster Unionist Harry West. By that time, Sands had been on hunger strike for 40 days.

Oliver believes that Sinn Fein and the IRA also failed to learn important lessons from 1980, with tragic consequences in the short term, but in the longer term the election victory proved extremely valuable. He contends that it turned Sinn Fein into an effective political machine, something the government failed to recognise. Moreover, the victory and the deaths that accompanied it made, in his view, a mockery of government attempts to present the prisoners as common criminals. This made the hunger strikes, in Oliver's view, the moment the British unwittingly lost the war against the IRA.

> In the euphoria of their election victory, Sinn Fein [sic] believed neither the British Prime Minister nor the British parliament would ever allow an MP to starve to death. That, in my opinion, showed that they too had failed to learn the lessons of the 1980 hunger strike. ... they seriously misjudged the will of the Iron Lady. I can recall Mrs Thatcher when she made it abundantly clear there would be no granting of political status for anyone who was serving a prison sentence for crime. "Crime is crime is crime. It is not political, it is crime," she said. Thatcher was impervious to international or high-level appeals for compromise.
>
> But Sinn Fein did learn [something] from the election victory. They learned how to campaign and win, and they built on that particular lesson. At the same time, the British government failed to recognise or acknowledge that Sinn Fein/IRA had moved onto the political stage.
>
> Although she won the battle of the hunger strikes, Thatcher and the British government really lost the war against the IRA at that point

in time. It was only a temporary victory for both the British and the Unionists. How could Thatcher maintain her claims the IRA were drug-dealing, racketeering gangsters? Gangsters and thugs don't starve themselves to death for an ideal, do they?

Oliver believes the hunger strikes of 1980-1 achieved far more for the IRA that its stated objective of political status for its prisoners. He contends it achieved far more than the IRA could ever have realised. In his own words, the IRA hunger strikes "opened the way for the endgame in Ireland".

Working with Oliver over many years in the intelligence field in Northern Ireland was "Coalface". Both men were aware of the intense rivalry between MI5 and MI6 in 1980-1. They share the view that MI6 wanted and indeed had primacy on intelligence matters in Northern Ireland at that time. MI6, for their part, viewed themselves as the more sophisticated and professional. This superior attitude gave rise to a widespread perception that MI6 were the better of the two agencies. Coalface and Oliver do not share that view. Instead they believe MI6 were controlled by status, cronyism and class and therefore were far less competent than the home-based service, MI5.

The opinion of both men is that MI6, being interested in a broader world-wide picture and because of sympathetic figures within the political administration at that time, had been allowed to usurp control of intelligence-related matters in Northern Ireland. Figures around the PM, in their opinion, were able to exert too much control over intelligence-related issues. Politics rather than practicalities were dominant. It has been further suggested that at least two of Thatcher's ministers were members of MI6.

Given MI6's involvement, the question arises as to what extent the security services kept a watching brief on Irish-American contacts. However, neither Coalface nor Oliver believe it was a major concern at that time. Both claim Sinn Fein had little if any political clout or status in the US then, a scenario that only changed in the aftermath of the hunger strike when the IRA realised and utilised its newfound status on the global political stage.

The international dimension that did exercise minds at the time was the location of Ireland in relation to East-West divisions. Ireland, being on the western extremity of Europe, held a strategic importance that has never been fully recognised. MI6 did have major concerns regarding IRA contacts with communist groups and were aware of ongoing contacts between such groups and the IRA. There was interest in what relationships would develop, if indeed any.

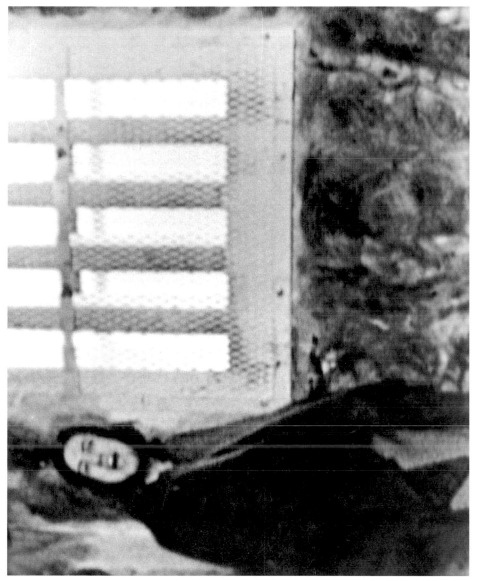

H Block Dirty Protest

Hunger Strike Demonstration

Funeral of Bobby Sands

Funeral Of Joe McDonnell

Rioting at Divis Flats

Long Kesh Prison Hospital Cell

Gerry Adams

The Hunger Strikers

Annual Hunger Strike March

Coalface believes MI6 feared the development of a strong IRA link with the Soviet Union. There was a fear that, in return for weapons and the like, the IRA would be willing aid and abet Soviet espionage against the British. A case of the enemy of my enemy is my friend, so to speak. A small espionage network or footing in Ireland could have provided the Soviets with a platform beyond the iron curtain and a stepping-stone for future use in Western Europe.

Coalface states, in his opinion, a great deal of unnoticed intrigue was carried out on the British side at that time by the late Ian Gow MP (a close friend of Thatcher and ardent Unionist supporter, assassinated by the IRA in 1990), a significant and much underestimated political figure at time of the hunger strikes. Coalface believes Gow's role in events has never been fully revealed. As a close ally of Thatcher, in the event of failure Gow would take the majority of political fallout and not the PM. Coalface further alleges that former NIO Secretary Atkins was MI6, and knew precisely what the intelligence agency was promoting at that time within the Republican movement.

Both Coalface and Oliver claim to have had no doubt that MI6 was the driving force behind the collapse of the hunger strike. They contend that the intelligence service had 'sleepers' inside the Republican movement and the Maze/Long Kesh prison. These sources kept them up to date with the situation inside the IRA and developments within the prison. This information, they claimed, was instrumental in helping devise the Mountain Climber strategy. At this point, Coalface said he had worked as a prison officer inside the Maze/Long Kesh during 1980-1. His cover was simple and plausible: he was a former British soldier who had been serving in Ulster, had married a local girl, quit the army and joined the prison service. This was not an uncommon occurrence and the same cover was used to get 'plants' inside the RUC and the UDR at that time.

Coalface simply listened, watched and reported back – simple but very effective. Being a prison officer he could come and go throughout the Maze/Long Kesh complex. He worked in the Republican blocks and was able to keep his superiors up to date on the prisoners' mood, morale, and so on. Coalface says he was not alone in believing there were other 'moles' on the Republican and Loyalist wings of the Maze/Long Kesh.

At one stage he was told to pay particular attention to Hughes and the deteriorating health of McKenna. He remembers one particular NIO official visiting the Maze/Long Kesh to speak with IRA hunger strikers in the prison hospital shortly before the end of the 1980 strike. Coalface claims the official had told the hunger strikers of specific changes that could be made to the prison regime should they decide to call a halt to the strike. He maintains he did not know whether anything was given in writing at that time. Coalface admits he did know Oatley, the MI6 officer who handed over the alleged document, but refuses to discuss his role in the ending of the hunger strike.

The intelligence services, Coalface reveals, had regular updates on the health of McKenna every few hours. He says the decision to remove McKenna to the Musgrave Hospital military wing was made by the NIO on the advice of the intelligence services, and claims the decision was ratified at Cabinet level. The reasons for the decision, Coalface believes, were twofold: one to ensure McKenna did not die; the other, more importantly, to ferment doubt and concern within the ranks of the other hunger strikers still inside the Maze/Long Kesh. Could they let McKenna die if concessions were just around the corner? Should they wait and see what was on offer. Coalface describes the manoeuvre as "blatant political brinkmanship".

Coalface claims to have been in no doubt that the British had assessed the hunger strikers were beginning to waver, and that the time was right to put on the pressure. He believes the much-heralded document was a political tactic designed to end the strike in favour of the British. Both he and Oliver insist the Thatcher government never had any intention of capitulating in the face of Republican demands. Coalface recalls that as being a fatal blunder:

> We had a clearly identified strategy within the intelligence sphere. It was watch, wait, assess and act – that's what we did. When the time was right, misinformation was put into the minds of the hunger strikers. McKenna was taken out of the Maze. We watched, waited, assessed and – when the time was right – turned the screw and it all collapsed. But it wasn't a long-term victory for the British government. Within weeks, it all backfired and they are still reaping the bitter harvest they sowed at that time.

From another arm of the British intelligence community comes Martin Ingram. He came to the public eye as a whistleblower on the Force Reconnaissance Unit, a shadowy section of the British Army that operated in Ireland from around 1982. Ingram was the handler of Freddie Scappaticci, the IRA's head of internal security who turned out to be a British agent run by the FRU. Ingram is not impressed with the Republican movement regarding the hunger strikes, and plays down their significance. His comments tend to suggest contempt for the Republicans' goals and methods, yet contain tacit acknowledgement that his organisation failed to anticipate the importance of the hunger strikes in furthering the Republican cause.

> I was a junior NCO. The hunger strikes were not a major issue to us at that time, from what I can remember. The focus then was really upon saving lives; i.e., of soldiers and policemen. The importance of the hunger strikes from an intelligence point of view was only really after the event; i.e., as a means of placing pressure upon individuals.
>
> The feeling at the time was that the deaths of the hunger strikers were a complete waste of life and, moreover, were used by the broad Republican movement as cannon fodder to further the aims but without being honest about the aim. The lady was never going to bend, or at least not enough to allow Republicans to claim victory. And they knew it. Today I remain convinced that a lot of lives were wasted by others that had not the guts to do it for themselves, but were keen for others to do the donkey work. I suppose today's suicide bombers are in a similar position.

This view, that the prisoners were unwitting dupes or somehow coerced by manipulative IRA leaders outside was prevalent at the time but has since been strongly challenged, if not largely discredited, by the mass of evidence that has entered into the public domain over the last quarter of a century. Even within the Unionist or British contributors to this book, such a view would be the minority view. Nonetheless, it is adhered to by some.

Chapter Ten:

Comms from the inside

Having been outmanoeuvred by British intelligence during the first hunger strike, the prisoners went into 1981 knowing that the stakes had been raised. In such circumstances, as pointed out by Bik McFarlane, prison OC during the second hunger strike led by Sands, this time it would have to be a "fight to the death". McFarlane reflects that while that is indeed what transpired, and the British publicly claimed the IRA were defeated, very rapidly things began moving behind the scenes that demonstrated the reality of what the prison protest movement was achieving – a lot of which rested on the emerging strategy of mass protest.

As detailed in Beresford's *Ten Men Dead*, it was comms from McFarlane inside the H-blocks to Gerry Adams, a former prisoner now working on the outside, that formed a transfixing narrative of the hunger strikes, the personalities and issues involved. The dilemmas, the hard choices, the courage, humanity and leadership make for an extraordinary story. Comms, as we have seen, were notes ingeniously transcribed onto toilet paper, cigarette paper or other materials, all smuggled out of the prison in just as ingenious ways, utilising every conceivable orifice of the prisoners and their visitors.

The prisoners knew their every move was being watched, and were alive to the fact that British intelligence was attempting to spy on them. From the prisoners' perspective, the authorities' attempts to gather intelligence and influence Republican thinking in the H-blocks appeared, perhaps ironically, to offer a channel of negotiation of sorts. McFarlane recalls:

> We were aware that some prison officers seemed to have more clout than others. They seemed to have access to information beyond the norm. Like, maybe they would have expressed opinions that indicated that they were getting information elsewhere. We formed the view that these guys were working to an MOD briefing. We also uncovered

that some of them had relatives or mates in Special Branch. Sometimes they'd present us with various hypothetical scenarios, like: "What if this happened," or, "what would you do if ... ?" and so on. We knew we were being sounded out by various people, various agencies. They were clearly trying to develop intelligence on our political thinking and what we might do next. Certain governors would have had links to the MOD. One guard confirmed to me later that these things were going on. How structured these activities were, or to what degree they were private activities of individuals in Special Branch, prison staff, who knows?

On other occasions, a screw might say: "My mate in Special Branch says that if you do X, Y, or Z, then maybe this or that would happen." And we might have taken the opportunity to say back later something like: "Well, if that's what your mate thinks, he's sorely mistaken, because we'd never consider doing X, Y or Z. So your mate would need to think again." And then later on, another scenario might be presented to us that obviously had taken on board the previous encounter. I suppose that was a channel of sorts, but I don't think a very structured one.

McFarlane had been chosen by Sands to succeed him as OC. Sands said all decisions regarding the progress of the hunger strike should be in the hands of non-hunger strikers: McFarlane as prison OC, with Danny Morrison and Gerry Adams as advisers on the outside. Whether he liked it or not, McFarlane was catapulted to centre stage in one of Ireland's most searing political dramas. McFarlane had asked to be allowed to join the hunger strikes on several occasions only to be told that the reasons for his being sentenced to 25 years in jail would be used as propaganda against the protests.

McFarlane had been jailed for his part in a bomb and gun attack on a known UVF haunt, the Bayardo Bar, on the Loyalist Shankill Road. The intended victims that day in August 1975 were members of the UVF who were at that time engaged in a sectarian murder campaign against Catholics. What had been conceived as a revenge attack for an earlier UVF strike on an Ardoyne bar in fact claimed the lives of five Protestants, only one of whom was associated with the UVF. McFarlane had been the driver of the IRA vehicle used in the operation.

Residual concerns over this operation precluded McFarlane's direct participation in the protest, yet he became a vital component in the Republican hunger-strike machine during 1981. Having witnessed the duplicity of the British in the ending of the first strike, and sharing the anger of the other prisoners at this, McFarlane was in no doubt Sands would see his fast through to the ultimate conclusion. In contrast to 1980, when all seven prisoners went on hunger strike at the same time, this time there would be a two-week interval between prisoners joining the fast. This allowed more time for negotiations and ensured the strike would continue well after the first deaths, should there be any, thus ensuring a greater build-up of pressure on the authorities. McFarlane remembers:

> The stakes were high and everyone knew this. Criminalisation was the big agenda for the Brits. So we knew they wouldn't back down easily, if at all. It was a calculated attempt to criminalize the whole struggle. The strategy of criminalisation was to hit Republican morale, to alienate us and to crucify us. In the Brits' war against Republicans, the softest option was always the prisoners.
>
> The defining moment had already been reached, so we knew now that this time it was "to the death". I became OC in January 1981. Bobby Sands had been OC but once you went on hunger strike you couldn't remain OC. Our analysis had not changed from the first hunger strike. We'd tried every conceivable protest, so the Brits had to know that we were serious. We had tried to steer clear of hunger striking but it wasn't possible in the end.
>
> [However] there was a confidence among the Blanketmen that we'd achieve the five demands. We knew that there'd be support across Ireland, in Europe, in the US. We knew that from the anti-H-block campaign, the Relatives Action Committees, the Troops Out movement, and so on.
>
> These various disparate parts were brought together by people who understood how important it was to maximise the protests. The communication we had between ourselves and the leadership outside was phenomenal. We used "comms". For instance, a message could go out the prison at 10 am, be replied to from the outside and then another reply sent from inside all in the same day. When the strike started, we ended the no-wash protest and then we got newspapers and stuff like that.
>
> The Irish Commission for Justice And Peace's efforts to end the strike really represented the Irish establishment's way of ending the protests.

You know, like the Church, the SDLP, the southern government, etc. And any offers that they said had been made by the British to end the strike were seen in that light. For instance, their views on "offers" would have a positive gloss on them. We wouldn't have shared their views on these things.

As well as voicing the hostility of Republicans to what they perceived as the disingenuous position of the ICJP, notwithstanding the sincerity of some of those involved, McFarlane also reflects the anger and betrayal felt by Republicans at the reluctance of the Haughey administration in Ireland to offer genuine support to the hunger strikers. "There were no direct talks with the Irish government," he insists. McFarlane believes this lack of support was based not only on a fear of incurring the wrath of Ireland's powerful next-door neighbour and opening a door for the Troubles in the south, but also on a fear of creating electoral competition for Fianna Fail by appearing to back northern Republicans.

The Taoiseach, Charlie Haughey, was more concerned with maintaining his own position than fighting the British for a deal for the prisoners. Why get in the ring with Mike Tyson when you don't have to? We were a much easier target. A much softer option. It made his life easier by not taking the Brits on, for all his rhetoric. Fianna Fail grassroots loved him ... But he gave a silver teapot to Thatcher when they met.

He'd say whatever he thought would get him off the hook. He actually said to the Sands family that the European Court of Justice would be an option. But he didn't tell them there was something like a five-year waiting list. And Bobby Sands was on hunger strike. But he had other reasons for not fighting our corner. He feared an upsurge in radical Republican politics, which would have offered an alternative to Fianna Fail and the rest. And if he had of been supportive of the five demands, then he might have attracted a number of radical voters. Voters who haven't previously voted tend to be attracted by something different, something more radical than what went before. That's why some non-voters become voters. Maybe he didn't want that element getting involved politically at all. Many of our natural supporters didn't vote. I think Haughey thought that if they started voting, they might want more and more radical change.

The Irish establishment also had a fear of events becoming polarised and running out of their control. This would be at the expense of the "middle ground". So along with the Church, they just wanted to throw a wet blanket over the whole thing. They just wanted it all to end, regardless of whether we got the five demands or not. It wasn't just the fear of the Troubles spilling over the border, but also a fear of radical politics spilling over too.

McFarlane reflects on what he sees as the origins of this new radical politics, an engagement between Republican ideology and the broader civil-rights movement campaigning against discrimination and, ultimately, partition. Like many, he strongly rejects the interpretation that sectarianism was what motivated Republicans and Nationalists. Instead, he insists, the goal was justice, pure and simple, a reflection on the fact that Republicans, and especially the prisoners, believed they were engaged in a historic struggle to free themselves from colonial occupation.

Some people came to Republicanism from the civil rights. I know it was always called an IRA front by some Unionists. There were Republicans involved, as there were others. But why shouldn't Republicans have been allowed to be involved. Lots of different kinds of people were. Civil rights agitation came about because the system wasn't right. If you have two competing sides and you give one side all the power, then they will abuse that power. And that's what had happened. It was never a religious issue. It was misrepresented by the media as such. And they would say things like, oh you know, these people just can't get along.

It was really a colonial situation. If you control a country, you control the wealth of that country. Maybe it would have been different if we had of been black. Then people would have seen that it was nothing to do with religion, it was about discrimination. The plantation of Ulster played a major part in shaping the relationships on this island. Presbyterians were brought over and given the land of the native Irish, who were then forced to move to less arable land, often up hills, mountains and places like that. Places like Pomeroy are an example. That was the impact of the settlers being brought in. So it wasn't about religion. England stole this country and has never given it back.

Irish Home Rule came at the wrong time for the British Empire. The Empire was in decline. The Boer War was a disaster for them. Ireland

was the "back door to the Empire" at one time for the French and perhaps even for the Germans. So apart from "kinship" with "Ulstermen",
there has always been a self-interest agenda on the part of the British.

However, British attitudes did begin to change in the aftermath of the
mass movement that was energised by the hunger strikes in the early 1980s.
It was perhaps in the H-block cells themselves that the changes became
most palpable. It was slow, stuttering progress, but within a decade it was
becoming obvious to prisoners that the British position was thawing considerably – a development with major implications. McFarlane reflects:

Pre-1983, there was the lockdown: no free association, no access to
educational material, educational books. You could get all the Harold
Robbins you could want – all that sort of stuff, no problem. But nothing political and definitely nothing in Irish. You weren't allowed Irish
music. You were allowed to request musical instruments. I asked for a
bodhran; I got a guitar. There was no poetry. I had an old time Russian
revolutionary from 1917 sending me an edition of their poetry. But of
course it was swiped. You just weren't allowed stuff like that.

One time, while I was OC, I was in the governor's office for a meeting with him. And I saw a memo on a wall there saying that under no
circumstances were we to get any political books whatsoever. I memo-
rised the memo word for word and got the contents of it to the outside.
And a letter was sent to the NIO, quoting the exact same words. The
next time I was in that office, the memo was gone. And at the time we
were non-protesting (although non-conforming) prisoners.

Straight after the hunger strikes, Prior [James Prior, who had replaced
Atkins as Northern Ireland Secretary in September 1981] conceded
some things quietly. But I'd say from December 1986 onwards, we had
a lot more than the five demands. The regime was gradually relaxed in
the aftermath of the strikes. The anger was palpable. See, you need a
degree of co-operation for things to be bearable for anyone to live in.
That goes for screws, prisoners and governors. By 1990, conditions out-
stripped anything we could ever have envisaged when we were cooking
up the five demands.

I escaped from Long Kesh in 1983 and was captured and returned to
the Blocks in 1987. It was obvious that the whole atmosphere had been
transformed. At one stage, the NIO officials would deal directly with

the prisoners on certain issues. Like, they'd actually be in the same room with a prisoners delegation, with that delegation's OC. So they clearly recognised our command structure, another difference from before the hunger strikes. Pre-1983, the prisons had a policy of lock and control. After the escape of 1983, somebody somewhere obviously said: "We don't need murder and mayhem inside or outside the blocks [prison staff were being killed on the outside]." In all these organisations, there will always be enlightened elements. It just depends on who is in the ascendancy at the time. We still had to fight for things, but at least we had someone to communicate things to. And he'd often say: "OK, fair enough, I'll see what we can do."

There would be officials who wanted to show that they could deal with you. Maybe it was a feather in their cap, demonstrating to their superiors that they could resolve tricky situations and deal with people like us prisoners. Maybe it was a good career move.

You needed that [overall improvement in conditions] for some kind of peace of mind. You could construct your day when you could wake up in the morning and say to yourself: 'Today, I'm doing such and such.' It was like normalising conditions, to the extent that the screws could actually leave the door open.

Don't get me wrong. Everything that was conceded had to be struggled for. It wasn't just given. But we worked hard at it. We personalised the situation where we could, like calling screws by their first names. And I became "Bik" instead of prisoner number 742, or whatever. We worked hard on the human touch. No prison in the world can work without some co-operation. So that's why we became non-protesting but non-conforming prisoners.

We needed a more harmonious atmosphere for not only peace of mind, but also for developing our politics. It made it easier to keep up to date with current affairs and even for other things. Like we could ask a screw for something and they'd sometimes try to sort it out. And to be honest, it enabled us to communicate more freely as we effectively had freedom of association. We also got visits and parcels weekly. We were also segregated from Loyalist inmates around October/November 1982, I think, which we had asked for. Most of the five demands were conceded by stealth over the years, but the one that was never fully conceded was the restoring of remission lost over years of protest. We maybe got thirty per cent remission, but not all of it.

Some Republicans think that due consideration of electoral methods would have suggested itself even without the hunger strikes as the campaign seemed be "going stale". Some kind of dialogue, so goes this view, was inevitable. One source for this book puts it this way:

> Even without the hunger strikes that would have happened anyway. I think the 'popular support' issue was important. But that didn't necessarily mean elections.
>
> I think without the hunger strikes, Sinn Fein's progress would have been slower. Republicans wouldn't have contested it [the Fermanagh-South Tyrone by-election] without the hunger strikes and they wouldn't have won it without a hunger striker being on it. If Republicans hadn't contested the election, or if we'd lost it, some would have said: "OK we tried that. What else is there?" If Republicans couldn't have got a vote out when Bobby Sands was weeks away from dying, then when could they?
>
> I think it's obvious now that the election, as an event in itself, was something of a focal point. It did make people more confident about the support they had. That made Republicans think about broadening their support base. There were politically minded ones ready for it, anyway. They would have seen it as chance to mobilise public opinion. But there was a long way to go before you could say "peace process". The cease-fire was the start of the peace process for some. But I'd say the hunger strikes opened up a new front that came to be main front over time.

Chapter Eleven:

Ten stories

After the setback of 1980, the forces on the "new front" of the Republican campaign regrouped and prepared for a second hunger strike. This time it would be a fight to the death. Battle commenced on the fifth anniversary of the withdrawal of special status, March 1 1981, when the IRA prisoner OC, Bobby Sands, began his fast. By the time it was all over in October, the hunger strike had claimed the lives of ten Republican volunteers and left a crater on Ireland's political landscape.

Why did the hunger strikers offer their lives in return for recognition as political prisoners? And what had driven them in the first place to join the IRA or the INLA and take the actions that resulted in their incarceration? The testimony of former comrades reveals something of the spirit and motives of these men, whose sacrifice, whether one agreed with it or not, pushed the troublesome shared history of Ireland and Britain onto a new axis.

The leader of the hunger strike was also the first to die. Robert George Sands was born in the Rathcool area of Belfast on March 9, 1954. He was one of four children, with two sisters and a brother. After leaving School in 1969, Sands starting work as an apprentice coachbuilder. Rathcool was a predominantly Loyalist area and, in 1972 after the Troubles had been going for around four years, the Sands family were – in common with many families throughout Belfast – driven out of their home.

Sands was first arrested at the age of eighteen. Six months after his release, he was arrested again and sentenced to five years' imprisonment. He served three, and was held in Long Kesh internment camp in one of the Nissen Huts, Cage Eleven – a building made famous years later in the writings of Gerry Adams.

During a brief spell as a free man, Sands married his long-time girlfriend, Geraldine, and the couple had a son named Gerard. The baby's father was arrested for a third time in October 1976. During his earlier spell in custody,

Republican prisoners had been accorded Special Category Status, but his third arrest took place after the March 1 cut-off point. Along with all other Republicans convicted after that date, he was subject to the new regime, which treated all prisoners as criminals.

Sentenced to fourteen years, Sands had been part of an IRA active service unit (ASU) that firebombed a Dunmurray furniture store. Future fellow hunger striker Joe McDonnell was also in the same party and he, too, was arrested. The jail term handed out to all six members of the ASU was on the evidence that a handgun had been found in their car.

Sands started this sentence in a punishment block since, at the end of his trial, there was a fight between guards and prisoners after Sands had been beaten by one of the guards. When he came out of the punishment centre he immediately joined the blanket protest and, in 1978, became Press Relations Officer (PRO) for prisoners "on the blanket".

Conditions in the cells were extreme. To the guards and the their superiors, the notion that the Republican prisoners were POWs was completely alien. Nobody had been forced into blanket protests or no-wash protests, they argued, and any hardships the prisoners suffered in connection with their refusal to wear uniform and play by the rules accorded to other criminals was entirely predictable and of their own making.

Others have a different perspective on who was to blame for the suffering that prompted the prisoners to protest. Johnny Donaghy, a Republican activist at that time, witnessed conditions inside the Maze/Long Kesh in the run-up to the hunger strikes. He recalls:

> I remember one visit I had just before the hunger strike and I saw five South Derry prisoners who had been forcibly washed and shaved. Patches of skin were missing from their heads and faces. They looked terrible; like people out of the Nazi concentration camps. One of them was my own brother and I didn't recognise him until he sat down and spoke to me.

Even before the prison protests began, the reality of life for Republicans in custody was regular beatings, constant verbal abuse, freezing cold and inadequate food. Unionists and the authorities would claim that prison was where these men belonged, having waged "terror" against the state. Despite such conditions, or perhaps because of them, the prisoners grew in determination. Denying their political status in exchange for a let-up in prison brutality would have signalled acceptance that they were no different from common criminals, and such capitulation would have demoralised their core support. It would also be an insult to their comrades, both past and present. The protest was not just about the cloth that made the prison uniform, but the right to resist the criminalisation of their cause, whether in jail or on the streets.

Rightly or otherwise, the prisoners were prepared to sacrifice everything to assert their political status. When the no-wash protest (started as prisoners complained about being beaten as they went to the toilets) followed the blanket protest after demands for political status fell on deaf ears, the prisoners had to smear their own excrement on the walls of their cells with all the horrors that produced. Moreover, because wearing prison uniform was a quid pro quo of visits from friends and relatives, protesting prisoners had little or no contact with the outside world, unless they conformed. Their only method of communication was the comms.

As the deprivations, isolation and brutality went on hour after hour and year upon year, the impervious stance of the authorities over the protests for political status served only to deepen the prisoners' sense of injustice and strengthen their resolve. Indeed, the conditions conceived to break the prisoners in fact moulded some Republicans into men prepared to resist to the death.

The determination of Sands and his followers was scarcely appreciated by the prison staff on the ground, let alone the NIO or Downing Street. When the prisoners released a statement on February 7 stating that they were resuming the hunger strike because the settlement agreed in December 1980 had not been adhered to by the authorities, the same forces that had conspired in December's defeat could not comprehend what it really meant. They were initially of the opinion that having been demoralised, so thought the authorities, the prisoners would not have the stomach for another long, debilitating hunger strike. The authorities further imagined that the public would soon tire of the issue. But, having been weathered by years of protest, the prisoners' mindset was one conditioned to struggle, every hour of every day. These prisoners had determination of a unique sort, built up and honed in to an extremely fine degree. The years of protest had fortified the prisoners and given them the strength for the final steps they were embarking on in the spring of 1981.

Paradoxically, there was also some difficulty in seeing things from the prisoners' point of view among the Republican leadership on the outside.

Fearing the consequences of failure, the leadership were initially resistant to the second hunger strike. Contrary to much anti-strike propaganda of the time however, the prisoners were the driving force behind the strike and it went ahead.

Sufficiently aware of the hardships the men on the inside were enduring and, determined to prevent a disastrous schism, the leadership knew overruling the prisoners was even more risky than letting them go ahead. What if the men, or some of them, decided to go on hunger strike anyway? Without official unity, it could be a disaster. Assent was therefore reluctantly given, and the outside leadership focused on working with the inmates. Again, the hunger strike was mounted in pursuit of five demands that recognised the prisoners' political status: the right not to wear a prison uniform; the right not to do prison work; the right of free association with other prisoners; the right to organise their own educational and recreational facilities, plus visits and parcels; full restoration of remission.

Sands and the leadership decided that instead of one mass movement, as in the first strike when all seven men joined at the same time, this campaign would be staggered. One man would start, with a new prisoner joining each fortnight. This would elongate the whole hunger-strike period for maximum political advantage should the worst happen and the British let hunger strikers die.

On the day after Sands made his move, Republican inmates called off their blanket protest to focus on the hunger strikes. On March 3, Northern Ireland Secretary Atkins restated to the Commons the British government's resolve to continue criminalising the prisoners.

Sands was a natural leader, and respected by the other prisoners. He had taken over as OC from Brendan Hughes in October 1980, when Hughes went on the first hunger strike. Sands was also a realist. Knowing that a second hunger strike would most likely be to the death, he had attempted to make the best of the "deal" the prisoners thought they had secured with the authorities in December. But the prisoners felt, over the first two months of 1981, that the authorities were simply humiliating them with each prevarication and disingenuous discussion. Entreaties from churchmen, southern political figures and other constitutional Nationalists to avoid a hunger strike were, meanwhile, viewed suspiciously. After all, from the prisoners' perspective, these forces had not helped during the first hunger strike. A gruesome period ahead was assured.

For the first seventeen days, Sands kept a diary of his hunger strike but eventually found it was taking too much out of him. He was a writer of considerable talent and, during his brief period of freedom in the mid-70s, had edited and distributed his own leaflet for the Twinbrook area where he lived. During his imprisonment, he wrote poems along with articles for Republican News under the pen name of Marcella. Marcella was the name of one of his sisters and was also the name by which he signed his comms.

Sands had a capacity for turning memorable phrases. One mural on a Belfast wall records his statement that: "Everyone, Republican or otherwise, has their part to play." In his diary's opening entry, the gravity of his situation is poetically expressed: "I am standing on the threshold of another trembling world". He was under no illusion as to the likely outcome of his actions, and regardless of one's political outlook, his courage cannot be denied.

Sands had decided that any negotiations regarding the hunger strike's progress would be handled by his replacement as OC, Bik McFarlane, in conjunction with the other prisoners. The thinking behind the transfer of authority was obvious. As the protest went on, the hunger strikers would naturally deteriorate physically and mentally, thus rendering them less effective in any negotiations with the authorities. Sinn Fein leaders Gerry Adams and Danny Morrison on the outside would also be heavily involved, since they possessed an overview of the situation that was denied the prisoners in their relative isolation.

The authorities meanwhile felt they had no reason to fear a different outcome from that which they had engineered in December. Then, on March 5, just a few days into the second hunger strike, everything suddenly changed with the unexpected death of Frank Maguire, independent Republican and MP for Fermanagh-South Tyrone. To paraphrase one of Gerry Adams's interrogators from the 1970s, "all bets were off". Maguire's tragic passing triggered a by-election in an area with strong Nationalist sympathies. It was viewed as untimely in more ways than one, by some.

After some Republican discussion, again over the risks of possible failure, convicted IRA prisoner Sands was put up for election. Standing as an anti-H-block and Armagh Prisoner candidate, and with a growing mass-awareness campaign supporting his hunger strike, Sands won the election on April 9 with 30,492 votes. It was a major setback for the British, with former Ulster Unionist Party leader Harry West defeated in a bitter and bloodstained contest.

Two days before the ballot, an IRA member in Derry shot dead Joanne

Mathers, a government census-taker collecting forms on a Nationalist estate in the city. She had expressed some fear to a Sinn Fein member living nearby (who was later exposed as a British spy) who assured her she should be safe, as she only had a few more doors to do. Mathers was married with a small child and worked part-time to make some extra money. She was killed by a Republican gunman from the Waterside area of Derry on the doorstep of a house that was one of the last she had to visit. Another IRA man, who was also giving information to the British at the time, reported that members of his IRA unit were "disgusted" by the killing.

If such a killing provoked disgust among IRA members, Unionists were enraged. This, they claimed, was what they were fighting all along. When Sands two days later won the election, many Unionists considered that the Nationalist constituency had voted for murder. However, many also remembered that ongoing killings by British security forces and Loyalist paramilitaries were no less brutal. To take one example from six days after the election, Paul Whitters, a fifteen-year-old boy, was killed by the RUC with a plastic bullet. He was shot in the back of the head from close range after a minor disturbance in the city, and died ten days later in hospital.

Despite its controversial circumstances, Sands's election victory suddenly gave the hunger strikes major political momentum. His campaign had been boosted by the three other men who had begun fasts in the intervening period. Francis Hughes commenced his on March 14, followed a week later by INLA member Patsy O'Hara from Derry and IRA man Raymond McCreesh from South Armagh.

Many thought initially that the mandate won by Sands would encourage Thatcher to examine ways of ending the protest. After all, this was not a Sinn Fein candidate – someone once removed from the battle, so to speak – that had won this seat. It wasn't a former Republican and it wasn't a suspected IRA man against whom nothing had been proven. This was a convicted IRA prisoner, one that had been on the blanket protest for years and who showed no "remorse" for his "crimes". The Thatcher government's response was to repeat that they did not speak to "terrorists". Furthermore, the law was changed so that no serving prisoner could in future stand for election.

Nevertheless, British propaganda that the IRA was finished and had played its "last card" now rang hollow in the ears of Nationalists. Sands had scored a tangible victory that impressed constitutional Nationalists and, of course, inspired Republicans. Buoyed by this success, expectations in the broad Nationalist community were high that, at the very least, the

British would have to engage in some sort of negotiation. Letting an MP die, thought Republicans and Nationalists, was surely not an option for the British government.

However, as time began to run out, it became clear to many that Thatcher was not for turning. On April 19, Bobby Sands MP received the last rites. The following day, representatives of the Irish parliament met with him as he lay dying in the prison hospital and, having failed to divert him from his course, tearfully left the room. They'd been accompanied by Sands's election agent, Sinn Fein member, Owen Carron. They also requested that Thatcher consider meeting them to discuss what was rapidly becoming a crisis. She rejected the idea the next day, stating: "crime is crime is crime. It's not political". It was a phrase that encapsulated the British policy of criminalisation.

This prompted Sands's sister, Marcella, to make an application to the European Commission on Human Rights on April 23, claiming the British had breached the European Convention on Human Rights regarding treatment of prisoners. Two days later, two European commissioners sought to see Sands in order to take his case forward. However, as Sands insisted that Sinn Fein representatives be present, the meeting was not possible.

Even the Pope's Private Secretary, Fr John Magee, who gave Sands a crucifix as a Papal gift, failed to move the hunger striker from his course when he attended his bedside on April 28. The following day, Magee also met Atkins and then Sands again, but to no avail. It was clear that Sands would see it through, and the British would not bend. With death now very near, on May 4, the European Commission stated that it could not proceed with Marcella Sands's application regarding the breach of Human rights legislation as it had no power to do so.

Bobby Sands died at 1.17am on May 5, 1981. As riots broke out throughout the north of Ireland, the political shockwave went around the world. Sands had been on hunger strike for sixty-six days. There were demonstrations in Milan, Paris, Athens and elsewhere. Several parliaments including those of India and Portugal, held a minute's silence for him (although in India, it was the opposition who stood, not the ruling Congress Party). The following day, it was reported that US dockworkers were to boycott British goods and several vigils were held by Irish Americans throughout the US. Thatcher's response was that Sands had chosen this course and responsibility could not be laid at the door of the British government.

At the funeral on May 7, 100,000 people paid their respects. Streets were subsequently named after Sands in France and Iran and he became a global household name. Meanwhile, as Sands's place on hunger strike was taken on May 9 by his comrade from the Dunmurray furniture store attack, Belfast IRA man Joe McDonnell, the world prepared itself for the next chapter in the drama: the fate of second hunger striker Francis Hughes.

On May 12, at 5.43pm, Hughes became the second to die. He had been on hunger strike for fifty-nine days. Once again, protests and riots followed. A few hours after Hughes died, Julie Livingstone, a fourteen-year-old Belfast girl, was shot by a British soldier with a plastic bullet during a protest she was not involved in. As army vehicles sped up the road to scatter the protest, the girl took cover with others behind a hedge, fearing for her safety. According to witnesses, she was shot from approximately five metres. The protest became a riot and young Julie Livingstone died the next day in hospital.

Hughes's death was destined to provoke bloody confrontation. He had already become a legend among Republicans. Operating from South Derry, his war against British forces had been an akin to a guerrilla campaign. He dressed in fatigues, was usually armed and on the run. There were tales of his having been spotted at a UDR checkpoint in a car yet waved through, the UDR personnel pretending not to recognise him because they wanted to avoid the inevitable gun battle. Hughes's reputation suggested he would not be taken without an almighty struggle. On another occasion, while finding himself surrounded by troops in a safe farmhouse while dressed in his IRA "uniform" of fatigues, he turned his clothing to advantage and, in the manner of a fellow British soldier, simply walked past the troops outside saying: "nothing here".

Men like Hughes saw themselves as soldiers in every sense. Whatever the rights and wrongs of his cause or the way he pursued it, Hughes's courage was indisputable – as was his ability to cause havoc and spread fear among the British Army and RUC. He was on a poster in every RUC station as Ireland's most wanted man and had displayed skill, tenacity and courage in evading capture and prosecuting his war – a fact grudgingly admitted by many of his foes and, indeed, by one of the prison staff interviewed for this book. Attempts to criminalize him – to brand him a terrorist, a gangster, or murderer – were bound to meet indefatigable resistance. Eventually captured by the British in March 1978 after a gun battle with two SAS men, one of whom he killed, Hughes was sentenced to life imprisonment and immediately joined the blanket protest. He also volunteered for the hunger strike of October 1980.

From Tamlaghtduff, near Bellaghy in County Derry, Hughes was born on February 28, 1956, the youngest of ten siblings. It has been said his involvement with Republicanism stemmed from when he was badly assaulted by British troops as he and his friends returned from a local dance. However, some other catalyst would have no doubt awakened his militancy since Hughes was the product of a rural area steeped in Irish history and a long tradition of armed resistance to perceived British imperialism.

With two men now dead, the pressure on both sides increased as the condition of other hunger strikers became critical. Cardinal Ó Fiaich sent Thatcher a telegram on May 13 pleading with her to intervene, but to no avail. The next day, Hughes's replacement on hunger strike Brendan McLaughlin, a member of the IRA, started his fast. Meanwhile, the death toll on the streets began rising – and over the course of the hunger strikes, over sixty people outside the prison would be killed.

On May 19, a landmine in Camlough in South Armagh, the home village of hunger striker Raymond McCreesh – now close to death – exploded under an army Saracen, killing five soldiers. A few hours after that, a twelve-year-old girl, Carol Ann Kelly, was shot dead by a British soldier near her home. An army vehicle had entered the Nationalist estate as the child returned from a shopping errand when one of the soldiers shouted that they were going to "get one of them" in revenge for the Armagh attack. There was no disturbance near them at the time when shot rang out and hit the girl. One of the soldiers jumped out and shouted back at his colleagues: "It's just a little girl!" He dropped his weapon and tried to administer first aid, prompting a reprimand from his commander. Carol Ann Kelly died two days later in hospital.

Four other civilians were killed by the security services with plastic bullets during the hunger strikes. These were Henry Duffy on May 22, Nora McCabe on July 8, Peter Doherty on July 24 and Peter McGuiness on August 9.

Two days after the attack on the British Saracen in his home village, May 21, McCreesh died at 2.11am after sixty-one days on hunger strike. He was followed that night, at 11.29pm, by O'Hara. They were replaced on hunger strike by IRA man Kieran Doherty and INLA member Kevin Lynch respectively.

Born in Camlough on February 25, 1957, McCreesh had been an active Republican in South Armagh since he was sixteen. He was arrested on June 25 1976 along with another IRA man, Paddy Quinn, after attempting to attack a British observation post. A further member of the team, Danny McGuinness, was arrested the following day while another escaped capture altogether. In March 1977, McCreesh received a fourteen-year sentence for attempted murder among other offences and he joined the blanket protest. His brother, Fr Brian McCreesh, regularly took Mass in the jail and as Raymond would not wear prison uniform, a condition for visits, Fr Brian was the only member of his family to see him during his sentence until he took a visit in February to tell his family in person that he was going on hunger strike.

Like his brother, Raymond McCreesh was devout in his faith. Along with other Blanketmen, he was beaten severely by prison staff but this simply stiffened his spiritual resolve. Culture had played a part in steeling McCreesh, too; he had been a keen history student at school and spoke Irish fluently. He had also been an IRA operator whose determination and skill had overcome his relative youth to command respect.

However, McCreesh had a quiet exterior that led others to sense signs of weakness. British intelligence constantly attempted to monitor the prisoners during the blanket protest in an effort to ascertain whom they thought was most likely to succumb to some "initiative" or other designed to split the prisoners and sap morale. McCreesh's outward calm appeared to fit the psychological profile of a candidate fit for "breaking", erroneously of course.

In the wake of Hughes's funeral, a curious episode occurred that was partly related to this "weakest link" notion. A journalist asked another brother of McCreesh whether there was any truth in a rumour that he was ending his fast. McCreesh was in a bad way at this stage but remained determined to stay on hunger strike until the five demands were met – relaying this position to his family at his bedside. But later that day, after the family had departed, they received a call from the prison saying they should make their way to the hospital again. They were told that there had been a "major development".

Apparently, McCreesh had been asked by a doctor if he wanted to come off his hunger strike by taking some milk. As Fr Brian talked to his brother, it became clear that the hunger striker was confused, which he himself acknowledged. On a following visit the next morning, a plaster was noticed on McCreesh's arm. Fr Brian and others concluded that McCreesh was being given drugs, which contributed to his disorientated state. Whether these were part of a treatment or not is unknown but many suspected it was a deliberate ploy to chip away at a perceived weak point in the hunger strike.

There were other instances which, when added together, suggested that there may have been a concerted effort to get McCreesh off the hunger strike. For instance, the notion that McCreesh was not determined to see it through was suggested in briefings to the British media – briefings which, with some exceptions, resulted in government propaganda being parroted without question. Such briefings were designed to confuse the Republican support base. It was even hoped that their negative effects would impact on the prisoners. On top of the press briefings, moreover, was a visit to the McCreesh home by a British Army patrol seeking to find out if an IRA funeral or non-military funeral was being prepared.

To Republican insiders, these seemed obvious attempts to unsettle the family and therefore bring pressure to bear on the hunger strike. McCreesh's fellow prisoners took none of it seriously and instead it was clear to many that dirty tricks were being deployed. McCreesh's closest supporters remained defiant. As though in retort to Thatcher's refrain that "Crime is crime is crime", Fr Brian was unequivocal: "My brother is not a criminal".

McCreesh was followed to the grave hours later by O'Hara, leader of the INLA in the H-Blocks. He, too, had been radicalised from a young age. Born in Derry city, at the age of fourteen O'Hara was shot in the leg by the British Army. He witnessed harrowing scenes as civil-rights marchers were beaten up by the RUC and B-Specials, and his elder brother was interned in 1971. It was an anti-internment march through O'Hara's native Derry that ended with the Bloody Sunday killings.

These incidents energised an O'Hara family history of Republicanism to propel the future hunger striker into a life of militancy. He was arrested and interned in 1974 and, after his release the following year, joined what was then the newly formed IRSP – of which the INLA was the military wing. The INLA first entered mainstream public consciousness when, in 1979, it killed Conservative MP Airey Neave. Neave had been a former war hero and intelligence officer who was expected to become Thatcher's Northern Ireland Secretary. A former POW himself, he had escaped Colditz and was presumed to be planning a hard-line security policy on Irish matters. His INLA assassination, carried out by car bomb in the car park of the Houses of Parliament in Westminster, was shocking in its audacity.

O'Hara had been active in the INLA at the time of Neave's assassination, having spent the late 1970s in and out of custody. Arrested in 1976 for possession of weapons, he was released after four months on "remand" – a period reflecting the fact that an unofficial type of internment was still being implemented under the guise of criminalisation. The authorities saw this as a way of taking terrorists off the streets; many Nationalists saw it as an infringement of civil rights. O'Hara had also been arrested in June 1977 in the south after holding a Garda at gunpoint. He was acquitted of the charge.

In May 1979, O'Hara was arrested again. He was later convicted and sentenced to eight years in prison. Once in the H-blocks he went on the blanket and, having demonstrated his ability and willingness to resist criminalisation, he surprised none of his close associates when he volunteered for hunger strike.

When O'Hara's body was returned to his family, they noticed that someone had inflicted burns on his remains. Some concluded that they were cigarette burns. It was also noticed that his nose had been broken. The treatment of O'Hara's body testified the extent to which some on the Unionist side detested Republicans, even dead ones. Again, this only served to harden further the will of the prisoners to resist criminalisation.

Two days after O'Hara's death, the IRSP won two seats on Belfast city council in the local government elections. People's Democracy, who also campaigned for the prisoners, won a further two seats. Former SDLP leader Gerry Fitt lost his seat largely as a result of the swing towards prisoner-supporting candidates.

The deaths of O'Hara and McCreesh were also followed by serious rioting. Again, Cardinal Ó Fiaich seriously criticised the attitude of the government. Four days later, on May 26, IRA hunger striker McLaughlin was forced to come off due to medical complications including internal bleeding. Like the others he, too, was replaced; in this case two days later by Martin Hurson, an IRA member from Co Tyrone. With a seemingly inexhaustible line of volunteers ready to take the place of the dead, it seemed for a moment that there was no end in sight.

However, on the same day, May 28, ground began to shift. In an apparent attempt to bolster flagging Unionist morale in the face of the hunger strikes' growing political momentum, Thatcher flew to Northern Ireland.

Having already gained a measure of mainstream political legitimacy by winning British elections, Republicans upped the stakes again by putting forward, on May 29, nine candidates for the forthcoming Irish general election. All were Republican prisoners, four of them hunger strikers. With the issue of the hunger strikes dominating Irish political life, this development was greeted with hostility by many in the southern Irish establishment.

They sensed that their long-standing fear of the Troubles spilling over the border was being realised. Three days before the southern Irish general election, on June 8, IRA prisoner Tom McElwee started his hunger strike. A tense contest was guaranteed.

Prior to the election, the Irish Commission for Justice and Peace had stated on 3rd June 1981, that they believed that a solution to the crisis could be found based on improved prison conditions, association and a "fudge" on work. Their intervention was of significance in country with a high percentage of mass goers. At a grass roots level, it kept the protest in the public eye (even if the media did not, as far as republicans were concerned) and added an element of moral authority absent in the minds of Catholics who abhorred IRA violence. Some might say that this was a demonstration of the Church fulfilling its moral duty. It certainly was concerned with saving the life of Joe McDonnell. The Nationalist community invested a lot of hope in the ICJP as a likely source of a compromise acceptable to all.

Republicans however saw this as a development fraught with danger. Though they too were determined to save lives, their tough stance was not without its own possibilities and they did not want their concentration on the five demands diluted by a softly softly approach of people who, however well intentioned, did not have Republican victory as their main aim. While the ICJP contended privately that the British authorities would not speak to the IRA, the IRA remembered that posture crumbling in 1972 and 1975 and during the 1980 hunger strike, when channels had been opened to facilities talks that were kept from the public. But they also knew that only a strong united front would make that a real possibility.

During the elections contested by hunger strikers or their supporters, an important role was played by the ICJP. While viewed with suspicion by Republicans, some suggested that the intervention of the ICJP helped broaden the issue from one of political protest to one of humanitarianism. The commission had been set up by the Catholic Church in 1970 to consider issues of human rights, peace and justice. Given that the issue of "humanitarianism" has more neutral connotations than the phrase "Republican protest", or even "prison protest", it made voting for anti-H-block candidates easier to square in the minds of many.

The general election in the south was initially inconclusive. Haughey's Fianna Fail were affected by an upsurge among some elements of the southern electorate for the anti-H-block campaign, which won two seats and came within a few votes of winning a third. In total, it took just over three per cent of the vote. This helped tip the balance towards Fine Gael and the Labour Party, who formed a coalition, pushing Haughey and Fianna Fail out of government. The election was the worst Fianna Fail result for twenty years, albeit there were other factors besides the hunger strikes for many voters. Taxation was a major issue and Fine Gael's policies in that regard were considered more attractive by many. Nevertheless, the issue of Irishmen dying in British jails for political status loomed large.

The two successful anti-H-block candidates were Paddy Agnew in Louth and hunger striker Kieran Doherty in Cavan-Monaghan. Joe McDonnell meanwhile came close in Sligo-Leitrim. During McDonnell's election campaign, his wife Goretti was, among many others, a tireless and effective spokesperson – often introducing the couple's children at campaign events, so determined was she to do everything possible to save his life. She believed winning the election in Sligo-Leitrim would put pressure on the Irish government to act. Maybe the British could afford to let its hunger striking MPs die, but surely not an Irish government. Republicans considered that the pressure brought to bear by anti-H-block prisoners winning in the south could, at the very least, be damaging for any southern government that failed to act.

On the 10th June, republican prisoners received another morale boost when news reached them of a daring escape of eight IRA prisoners from Crumlin Road jail. In an atmosphere laden with grief and anger, such news was a tonic for those continuing protests and as a reminder that even in jail, victories could be had.

Meanwhile, throughout June, Fr Faul was suggesting to McFarlane and others that the prisoners should "clarify" what they wanted as many people didn't know exactly what they might settle for. Also that the prisoners should be seen to be flexible. The name of John Hume (and O'Fiaich) was suggested as a "mediator". But the prisoners were insistent that they could speak for themselves. The government however was maintaining it's stance that it would not negotiate with the IRA.

The Northern Ireland Prison Minister was therefore duty bound to meet several times with the ICJP, who felt they were getting somewhere with him. However, his boss, Humphrey Atkins, stated publicly in June that there could be no improvements in conditions or discussions at all until the hunger strike ended. With the approaching death of Joe McDonnell, the British were digging in. The ICJP requested a meeting with Atkins. It was noted by some that the ICJP were meeting with the press, the Irish government, the NIO, even the RUC, but not thus far with the prisoners.

On 15th June Fr Murphy sought the prisoners view on the ICJP initiative. He was told by McFarlane that it did not reflect the prisoners' idea of a basis for a settlement.

No annual Bodenstown commemoration for Wolfe Tone, the Protestant founding father of modern Irish Republicanism, was held by Fianna Fail, which has as its subtitle, "The Republican Party". This was the first time in the parties' history that it did not hold such an event.

On the 2nd July the ICJP met with Atkins and but without any real hint of movement from the British side, the meeting was not the breakthrough an expectant Nationalist public had hoped for, although the ICJP were hopeful. However, when they met Atkins again on 4th July, the British line appeared to have hardened.

Cardinal O'Fiaich met Thatcher but not only was there no hint of compromise, there was no hint in O'Fiaich's mind that Thatcher actually understood the political situation in Ireland. She asked why was it that the Irish who, "always had a problem could not be friends while Germany and Britain could". His answer was, "because you no longer occupy the Ruhr". To a British Prime Minister who insisted that Northern Ireland was as British as Finchley (her own constituency in north London), this argument may have made minimal impact.

The ICJP met the prisoners inside the H-blocks on July 4, although OC McFarlane was not permitted to attend. In disrupting the Republican command structure, the authorities hoped differences might open up between the leadership of the IRA and the prisoners. Also, they were not prepared to legitimise the IRA by recognising its command structure. The same day, the prisoners issued a statement that they were not seeking privileges for themselves, and that any flexibility shown by the government need not necessarily be shown just to them. McFarlane was able to meet members of the commission the next day as "visitors". The ICJP suggested that some, though not all, of the prisoners' demands were achievable and that prisons minister Michael Allison had indicated some compromise might be possible. If so, the ICJP argued, it was worth considering since McDonnell's condition was by now rapidly deteriorating.

Hazardous similarities with the first hunger strike now became clear. The prisoners would have to decide whether to accept the British word that compromise was possible to save the life of a prisoner. Adding to the complexity of the situation, the ICJP were unaware that parallel discussions were taking place between the Provisional IRA and Sinn Fein leadership and the British agent "Mountain Climber".

It was said to Adams, via the secret channel, that a statement would be made in which all prisoners, not just paramilitary ones, would be able to wear their own clothes. Further, a compromise on prison work could be worked out, as could some of the remission lost by the prisoners on protests. Sinn Fein negotiator Morrison was allowed into the jail, as proof of British good intentions, to relate the initiative to the hunger strikers with McFarlane present.

With nothing in writing, the prisoners wanted confirmation the initiative had substance. As this initiative promise to deliver more than the ICJP one, Adams, who had been told that any breach of confidence would result in the proposal being withdrawn, took a calculated risk and informed the ICJP of the behind-the-scenes discussions so that they would not muddy the waters with their own talks with Allison. The prisoners were meanwhile told that an official from the NIO, authorised by the British, would go into the prison, meet them and give them confirmation of the initiatives that night, July 7.

The British official never did go in. Instead, the NIO said that there had been a change of plan and that the official would go in on the morning of July 8. Why the prevarication, asked the ICJP? The British may have believed O'Donnell would live through the night, based on their interpretation of the medical information before them. There has also been speculation of conflict in the British camp, between hawks and doves. Whatever the reason, the next morning turned out to be too late. McDonnell, a man who had initially been reluctant to volunteer for hunger strike because he believed he "had too much to live for", died at 4.50am.

Born on in the Lower Falls area of Belfast, on September 14 1951, McDonnell had been the fifth of nine children. In 1970 he married Goretti Healey, but the couple had to flee their first home after Loyalists kicked in their door and destroyed the house. In 1972, McDonnell was interned without trial. On his release he joined the Belfast Brigade of the IRA and was arrested at the same time as Sands when they firebombed the Balmoral Furniture Company in October 1976. By this time McDonnell had two young children.

McDonnell was known as fearless operator, discreet about his activities and all the more respected for that. Like Sands, the leader of the ASU on the Balmoral operation, he had been sentenced to fourteen years. He refused to wear prison uniform and, like the Blanketmen he joined, refused to be criminalized. Joining the hunger strike and seeing it through to the death, the circumstances surrounding his passing seemed to show the British at either their most determined, or at their most incompetent. Whether they misjudged the situation or realised that any concession would be a defeat for them, the loss of McDonnell was another key moment.

Inevitably, there were further angry protests and violence in the immediate aftermath. But there were also recriminations among Republicans, some of which have taken more than twenty years to surface. The IRA prisoners' press officer at the time, Richard O'Rawe, has recently claimed that in the days and hours before McDonnell's death an acceptable offer from the British had actually been made in return for calling off the hunger strike but it was never passed on to the hunger strikers. Had the Republican leadership done so, according to O'Rawe's account, McDonnell's life could have been saved. His version hinges on a discussion he claims took place in the H-blocks between him and McFarlane on Sunday July 5 in which a "deal" was discussed, approved by McFarlane but then overruled via a comm from the IRA army council outside.

This version of events is disputed however by just about everyone else who was involved at the time and by former OC McFarlane, who was at the centre of the chain of communication in July 1981. McFarlane insists that the Republican leadership acted honourably and that no acceptable offer was made by the British. McFarlane further testifies that the July 5 "discussion" described by O'Rawe never actually took place – McFarlane was attempting to gain access to negotiations in the hospital unit, and therefore was not in the H-blocks, at the time in question. This fact is corroborated by then Sinn Fein negotiator Morrison. Moreover, O'Rawe's version, published in his book *Blanketmen*, does not demonstrate that the British "offer" was written down nor that it was guaranteed in any way. McFarlane's view (and the view of the vast majority of people involved at the time) is that, without a written statement, anything that had to be taken on trust from the British after the "trick" of 1980 was categorically considered unacceptable.

Hopes of a settlement had been raised before McDonnell's death by the intervention of the ICJP and the conciliatory statement of the prisoners on July 4, but when McDonnell died without an agreement being reached it caused despondency among many.

ICJP initiatives had indeed offered some hope, but to many Republicans they were too much like giving in. Republicans feared the ICJP would settle for less than the prisoners would, or that they would oversell a weak British offer in an effort to bring the standoff to a conclusion. The prisoners were aware that the British would attempt to manipulate the moral authority of the Catholic Church, via the ICJP, in order to get a vague, indefinable – and retractable – deal accepted. Again, in light of the chicanery of December, Republicans had no faith in any British-backed initiative that was less than watertight. McFarlane recalls:

> There were various ICJP suggestions along the lines of, "What if this, what if that". In fact I remember Joe McDonnell being adamant that there was no real offer and that nothing less than the five demands would do. By now, men had died.

Republican resolve held firm through the critical circumstances of McDonnell's death and he was replaced on hunger strike by Pat McGeown from Belfast on July 9. The next day, McDonnell was buried. Rioting broke out at his funeral when the British Army attempted to apprehend a party of IRA guards that had fired over the coffin.

Having tracked the gunmen by helicopter, the security forces showed the government's determination to clamp down on the IRA at every opportunity. Funerals, with their attendant firing parties of IRA volunteers, gave the authorities a chance to demonstrate that there would be no let up in their battle against the IRA – not in jail, not on the streets and not at funerals.

Meanwhile, the number of protesters on the streets was beginning to grow thin. It was becoming clear to many that no amount of protesting would change the British government's mind, and a feeling of deflation set in.

On July 13, Hurson from Cappagh in Co Tyrone became the sixth volunteer to die after forty-four days on hunger strike. Hurson had joined the strike on May 29 as replacement for Brendan McLaughlin, who'd been taken of the fast due to medical complications. Hurson's rapid deterioration after forty days caused surprise since he had been considered more physically fit and strong than most.

Born on September 13, 1956, Hurson lost his mother to a sudden illness when he was thirteen. Arrested in November 1976 and convicted on the basis of a statement he insisted had been beaten out of him, he was sentenced to twenty years imprisonment for charges including IRA membership and attempted murder. Years later, four detectives who interrogated Hurson were charged with assault in relation to their questioning of James Rafferty, one of those arrested with Hurson.

Hurson appealed and was given a retrial, at which statements taken during his interrogation at Omagh RUC station were ruled inadmissible. However, statements made at another scene of further interrogation, Cookstown RUC station, were allowed despite allegations that they, too, were the product of police brutality. The appeal was unsuccessful.

Going on the blanket protest, Hurson was actually held in the young prisoners wing where under-eighteens were incarcerated. There were reports of brutality against prisoners in many blocks and the Young Prisoners wing was no different. A warder tried to break Hurson's leg by slamming it in a door, but this type of treatment failed intimidate or demoralise him and he volunteered for the first hunger strike of October 1980. He was kept on stand-by by OC Sands should one of the original seven men die.

After joining the second hunger strike, Hurson became a candidate in the Irish election in June. Winning 4500 votes in the Longford Westmeath constituency, once transfer votes were added he outperformed a Fine Gael and two Labour party candidates. On July 12, when Hurson began to deteriorate suddenly and unexpectedly, his family were called to the hospital unit. His fiancée, Bernadette Donnelly, was refused permission to see him as she was not considered family – even on the night before he died. The British claimed they believed he had more time but, unable to consume water, Hurson's descent was rapid and he died a particularly painful death. He was replaced on hunger strike the following day by IRA volunteer Matt Devlin.

On July 15, Atkins announced that the Red Cross had been invited to conduct an investigation into conditions in the H-blocks. The following day, a Red Cross delegation entered the blocks to discuss the situation with the prisoners. Atkins met the delegation the day after that, eager to cross-reference his existing intelligence with what the Red Cross had observed. It was as much a debriefing as it was an effort to resolve the situation.

The British were anxious that the deadly game might be slipping away. The Nationalist population was more alienated now than at any time since Bloody Sunday, if not since partition itself. As Atkins saw it, losing the hunger-strike battle now would leave the British with the worst of both worlds: with forty per cent of the population guaranteed to become more actively hostile either way, their authority would be effectively destroyed among the remainder if they opted to "cave in". Men were now dead. If the government capitulated now, so they thought, then they were open to the charge that they let men die for something that had been within their gift all along. Moreover, the Unionists would be outraged. The government, from their perspective at the time, had only one course of action to follow.

The British realised the greatest danger lay in being cast as the obstacles to a resolution. While that would not upset their natural supporters, remaining intransigent would make it more difficult for those elements in the international community who had chosen "non-intervention", such as the US, the EEC and others, to keep out of the affair. Further, such demonstrable inflexibility would alienate crucial elements in the SDLP who were becoming more vocal in their criticism of the hunger strikes and their destabilizing effect on society.

That weekend, on Saturday July 18, supporters of the hunger strikes demonstrated outside the British Embassy in Dublin. Given that it had been burned down after Bloody Sunday nine years previously, fears were high of a repeat. It was prevented this time around. The Gardai took a tough stance and hundreds of people were injured in violent clashes.

A few days later, an important new development took place. After the hunger strikers made it clear that casting the Red Cross in the role of de facto intermediaries between the prisoners and the government was not the answer to the situation, the Red Cross announced that their efforts had failed. On the same day, however, 23 July, the Foreign Office sought to reactivate the channel of negotiation with a communiqué. It suggested that the British were prepared to state that the prisoners could wear their own clothes, exchange parcels and have visiting privileges. Furthermore, twenty per cent remission would be restored. Free Association, however, was not on the table.

Granting free association would, in government eyes, be the most damaging concession since it did most to legitimise the political-prisoner concept – something they still roundly rejected. Free association would effectively hand control of the jails to the paramilitaries and the government's authority would be fundamentally undermined. It was the thin edge of a long wedge according to the authorities. Free association also facilitated the development of IRA strategy and tactics, which defeated the purpose of putting militant Republicans behind bars. Allowing "the enemy" such freedom under their very noses would be faintly humiliating to many in the British camp.

Nevertheless, some substantial concessions were apparently being offered. In addition to those already outlined was an assurance that Stanley Hiddich, the unpopular prison governor, would be moved on and his place taken by someone else. Another, as far as the government was concerned, was the very fact that they were even talking to the leadership of the IRA. This was considered a major concession in itself, bearing in mind the risks attached to such talks should they become public knowledge. Perhaps unsurprisingly, nothing offered by the British at this stage was in writing or otherwise guaranteed.

That being the case, the IRA leadership pointed out that even if they accepted the terms, there was no guarantee the prisoners would. The prisoners wanted their five demands met and, if there was to be a compromise, it would have to be guaranteed. This stance was prompted not only by British capitulation over an un-guaranteed offer in December 1980, but also by concerns that prison staff could "misunderstand" any ambiguous new regime. The deal had to have a guarantee. At this response, the British concluded the initiative, regretting that there was no resolution apparent. It was another frustrating false dawn.

There is the suggestion that, with some help from Taoiseach Fitzgerald, this period of "initiative" and the various to-ings and fro-ings that accompanied it was deliberately staged to collapse in such a way as to cast the British in a positive light and leave the prisoners appearing obstructive. A visit was made to the Maze/Long Kesh by some NIO officials who, once there, spoke with the families of Doherty and Lynch and then to the hunger strikers themselves. All insisted that OC McFarlane would have to be present to hear the "clarifications" from the British of various suggested resolutions. The NIO refused on the grounds that recognising the IRA command structure in prison would be to make a nonsense of the entire British position; it would call into question the illegality of the IRA, undermine the policy of criminalisation and compromise the sovereign authority of the British state to deal with what it considered to be a "domestic" matter.

The British were able to make this refusal knowing that the very fact NIO personnel had talked to hunger strikes allowed the government to present itself as having made a reasonable attempt to negotiate an end to the crisis. Prompted by this, Taoiseach Fitzgerald stated publicly that the British had done all they could and that the prisoners themselves were the obstacle to a solution. The propaganda battle raged on.

The British did not succeed in weakening the resolve of the prisoners, but their strategy had a corrosive effect on the morale of the prisoners' loved ones. On July 28, an attempt was made to call a halt to the strike by Fr Faul, who planned to invoke the authority of the prisoners' families to get the men of the strike. Motivated by religious and humanitarian concerns, Fr Faul was equivocally sympathetic to the hunger strikers' plight but his unwillingness to back their cause would soon earn him the soubriquet "Dennis the Menace" among Republicans. While an Irish Nationalist, he abhorred the methods of the IRA.

Fr Faul knew that the next of kin had the legal power to take the men off hunger strike once they lapsed into a coma. He arranged to meet the families at Toome in South Derry, where he gave his view that it was futile to continue as the British would not give in. Together, the priest and the families then drove to Belfast, where they met Gerry Adams and asked him to tell the prisoners to come off their fast. Adams initially informed them that he could not do that, but later phoned Fr Faul to say he was willing to go into the prison himself to talk to the prisoners about the options.

Thanks in part to the efforts of Fr Faul and others, the British government sensed victory was within its grasp. On July 29 members of the IRSP and Sinn Fein were given permission to visit the hunger strikers to suggest that a period of suspension of the hunger strikes might give them time to assess the various "reforms" or "initiatives" that had so far been suggested.

The delegation included Adams, along with Sands's former election agent and future successor as MP for Fermanagh-South Tyrone, Owen Carron, and Seamus Ruddy of the IRSP. With Doherty and Lynch by now too ill to attend, Adams outlined to the other six hunger strikers and McFarlane what was on the table. Adams made clear that any decision on what to do next was up to the prisoners themselves, and that the Republican movement would back them whatever they decided to do. At this stage, however, the prisoners believed ending the hunger strike was not the way forward. McElwee responded that if they gave up now, they would be made "to crawl".

The delegation then went with McFarlane to meet Doherty. Adams told the hunger striker that he would likely die; Doherty's response was: "I am not a criminal." Lynch was too ill to be disturbed. Lynch's father asked Adams why he did not take the prisoners off hunger strike. Adams replied that he could not, but that Lynch senior had the power to do so if he wished.

The mother of IRA hunger striker Paddy Quinn exercised just that option on July 31 by taking him off after 47 days of fasting. Quinn, from

South Armagh, had been on the first hunger strike for its last four days. Arrested in 1976 after the same operation that also saw McCreesh jailed, he was convicted of attempted murder and handed a fourteen-year prison sentence. During the run-up to the hunger strike, Quinn's brother Seamus had been taken to hospital with a life threatening kidney disease that turned out to be a hereditary condition. Paddy Quinn refused to be tested for the disease as he knew he was embarking on hunger strike. As his fast went on, however, Quinn had more and more trouble keeping water down – which was crucial to maintaining any kind of health while on hunger strike. His health deteriorated much quicker than anticipated and he was near death by the time his mother intervened.

That action opened a new phase in the hunger strikes, as the other families suddenly came under huge pressure. Should they let their sons die when they could intervene to save them? Or should they respect the fervent wished of their loved ones, and not take them off unless an agreement is reached? The Catholic Church was in no doubt that the families were morally obliged to intervene, and did its best to facilitate the move. Whatever the families decided, the Republican leadership made clear their wishes would be respected. Many Republicans felt the endgame was now in sight; an endgame that they stood to lose.

At 1am on August 1, Lynch became the seventh hunger striker to die. He had survived without food for seventy-one days and, in the end, his death was comparatively peaceful. Like Hurson, Lynch was born in 1956, on May 25. He was the youngest of eight children in a family that lived in the Co Derry village of Park near to where they later moved, Dungiven. Again, like Hurson, Lynch went to find work in England. He returned to Dungiven in August 1976.

Around this time, Lynch joined the INLA and in September he and three of his comrades held up an RUC checkpoint. Armed with only one shotgun between them, they disarmed four policemen – an incident that was retold many times in Republican circles. However, the RUC caught up with Lynch in December 1976 and he was held "on remand" for a whole year. He was subsequently sentenced to ten years and, on entering the H-blocks, immediately went on the blanket.

Lynch joined the first hunger strike in October 1980 until it was called of five days later. Ill-treatment by the prison warders only hardened his resolve to resist. He contested the Waterford constituency during the elections for the Dail in June 1981. Although he was unsuccessful, it was not a seat the H-block campaign had expected to win. The aim of the campaign was to keep the hunger-strike issue alive in another part of Ireland. He won a respectable 3337 votes before transfers. Though not enough to make Lynch a TD, such electoral support could not be written off given the concerted British attempt to portray each hunger striker as a criminal. Moreover, it further demonstrated that while there continued to be protests on the streets after each hunger striker died, electoral politics, regardless of whether the candidates would take their seats or not, was firmly establishing itself among the Republican movement.

While Kevin Lynch's mother expressed her relief that Quinn's mother's suffering had ended when she took her son, Paddy, off hunger strike, Mrs Lynch felt she had made a solemn promise to her own son that could not be broken. Lynch's place was taken on August 3 by another INLA volunteer, Liam McCloskey.

Attention now focused on Kieran Doherty, facing death unless an eleventh hour settlement could be found. Born on October 16, 1955, in Andersonstown, West Belfast, Doherty came from a staunchly Republican paternal family. His mother had been a Protestant who converted to Catholicism. By the time of his hunger strike, Doherty also had a steady girlfriend, Geraldine Scheiss, who had been unaware of Doherty's Republican involvement until he was arrested.

He had joined the IRA in March 1972, a time when many Nationalists in West Belfast considered it to be the only option in a city effectively at war. He had previously been a member of Na Fianna Eireann, the youth wing of the IRA. In February the following year, he was interned for two-and-half years. In August 1976, he was arrested and charged with possession of firearms and explosives. He and those arrested with him spent nearly a year and a half on remand. In February 1978, he was sentenced to twenty-two years in jail. He immediately went on the blanket and, in common with other prisoners, endured several beatings. Having joined the first hunger strike for its last five days, Doherty surprised nobody when he volunteered for the second.

As his fast entered a critical stage, it became apparent that Kieran Doherty TD would become the second elected representative die on hunger strike that summer. However, late on July 23, he asked family members at his bedside for "tablets", which seemed to indicate that he wanted to come off hunger strike. However, there had been occasions when other hunger strikers in an advanced state of physical deterioration became delirious, giving confusing signals regarding coming off hunger strike that turned out to be unrepresentative of their true wishes. Did Doherty know what he was saying, and if he didn't would he later resent being taken off? Was he really asking to come off hunger strike now after remaining steadfast for all this time? Faced with this dilemma, the family discussed the matter in conjunction with the doctor. They formed the view that Doherty had become delirious after many weeks without food, and agreed that his original wishes had to be respected.

On August 2, after 73 days without food, Doherty became the longest-serving hunger striker to die. In Dublin, flags flew at half-mast in respect of the fact that he was an elected member of the Dail. Later that day, near Omagh, an IRA landmine killed two RUC officers. In an attempt to trigger an end to the standoff, the prisoners reaffirmed four days later their concili-atory statement of July 4, reiterating that they were not looking for "elitist or preferential treatment".

By now many of the prisoners considered that the entire hunger strike protest was being taken out of their hands by "moderate" Nationalist forces trying to pressure the families into bringing their loved ones off hunger strike. Certainly, Fr Faul and other Catholic clerics who had become in-volved had inadvertently succeeded in splitting the families' united front. Some claimed that it would have happened anyway. Doherty's family had already decided they wanted nothing more to do with Fr Faul who, in their view, was working against the prisoners' true wishes by actively trying to break the strike. Under the influence of Fr Faul and other churchmen, however, there were now several families who were considering talking their loved ones off hunger strike when they lapsed into coma.

It was considered by the prisoners that the Church, the Irish government and the SDLP had all let them down by failing to support their demands and then actively seeking to end the strike by encouraging the families to intervene before a settlement was offered. Many Republicans viewed this as a betrayal. The British would be even less likely to consider a compromise seeing that the strike was collapsing, and would be encouraged by the fact that collapse was being facilitated by "moderate" Nationalists. The prisoners and the IRA would be seen as isolated. The Irish establishment claimed that there really was no chance of a settlement and that further deaths would not help anybody.

The following weekend was the tenth anniversary of the introduction of Internment, which, along with Bloody Sunday formed a chain of seminal moments to which the hunger strikes were now being added. With eight hunger strikers dead, two of them elected representatives, peaceful vigils had become regular events. Despite the fact that such vigils and protests were participated in by the broad Nationalist population, the fact that they were often organised by the anti-H-block campaign encouraged the authorities to characterise them as subversive Republican gatherings and attempt to break them up with force. The following example illustrates the process by which peaceful protests could become violent. Republican activist Johnny Donaghy remembers a peaceful vigil that he and others organised in Bellaghy after hearing of Francis Hughes's death on hunger strike back in May of that year.

> It was intended to be peaceful. It was organised out of respect for the Hughes family and to show support. We met in the centre of the town and then we were confronted by a group of DMSU [the District Mobile Support Unit] of the RUC. They would have been very aggressive, more aggressive than your normal "bobby" on the beat. In fact, many of these "bobbies" would be a bit resentful of these DMSU boys because they'd just come in and wreck the place and go on to their next place. And the "bobbies" would be thinking [in relation to themselves], one of us might get shot over what these DMSU people have done.
>
> At this vigil, the DMSU would have been ready, knowing as we all did, that Frances Hughes had died. And they'd be moving towards us with their batons raised, catching your eye and saying things like: "When this goes off, you are mine", and all that. Then, just when they were about to get really stuck in, an American TV crew arrived. So they couldn't get going at us the way they wanted to. And that was a response to a peaceful vigil.

Such heavy-handed provocation was precisely why so many protests and vigils ended in riots. At the same time, however, not all riots began as peaceful gatherings. There was real, renewed anger not only against the police, but also the entire state. It has been suggested that the IRA maintained a comparatively muted military response to the hunger-strike situation in order to tailor its energies towards clashes with the security forces on the streets; clashes that, in bringing the wider Nationalist community into direct and regular confrontation with the state and its enforcers on the ground, had the effect of radicalising a new generation of young men and

women from non-Republican backgrounds. As well as the dozens killed
outside the prison since the start of the hunger strike in March, more than
1000 people had by this point been injured and many more, approximately
1700, arrested by the authorities. This had the effect of radicalising many
families and communities.

Attention began to focus on the condition of McElwee, a cousin of
Hughes and also from Tamlaghduff near Bellaghy. Some of the prisoners began to decline under the intense pressure. Some were coming to the
conclusion that continuing wouldn't achieve anything. They felt that the
point had been made and that further protest was not going to move the
government, win any more support for the cause or even improve prison
conditions. However, the majority of prisoners wanted to continue; some
insisting that there should be no compromise under any circumstances
short of the five demands.

The sense that this was the latest stage in a historic struggle for freedom
remained acute in the minds of most prisoners, something those who sub-
scribed to the view that criminalisation would break the Republican spirit
never really grasped. Among those steeped in this sense of historic purpose
was McElwee. Born the fifth of twelve children on November 30, 1957, he
and his brother Benedict used to play with Hughes in the close-knit area of
south Derry. This was an area with a vibrant collective memory of struggle
against centuries of oppression under British rule. It was not the sort of place
likely to produce men who could be persuaded that militant Republicanism
was a criminal activity.

McElwee had been arrested on October 9, 1976, after a bomb that he
and others in an IRA ASU had been transporting by car in Ballymena, Co
Antrim, exploded prematurely. McElwee was the driver and the three others
in the car included his brother Brendan. Tom McElwee lost an eye in the
explosion, while his brother suffered a perforated eardrum. Another volunteer with them, Sean McPeake, lost a leg, while the remaining volunteer,
Colm Skullion, lost two toes.

In Tom McElwee's pocket, a list of targeted shops was found, one being
the Alley Katz boutique. A bomb exploded in this shop an hour after the
bomb in McElwee's car had prematurely gone off and, after a girl was arrested in connection with the incident, she named Dolores O'Neil – McElwee's
girlfriend – as her fellow bomber. Inside the shop, Yvonne Dunlop, a mother
of three, was burned to death despite the attempts of a local man – alerted
by the screaming of her son who told him his mother was still inside – to

save her life. A warning had been sent but, it was said, only ten minutes were given to clear the area. That was not enough time. The action was part of a commercial bombing campaign that had been planned by Dominic McGlinghey, an IRA commander in south Derry at the time.

After spending several weeks in hospital, McElwee was charged and sent to Crumlin Road prison. He was convicted of murder in September 1977, as well as possession of explosives. Both McElwee and his brother, also in the H-blocks, wanted to go on hunger strike in October 1980. Tom McElwee's determination to do so meant that when the second hunger strike came around there was little doubt he would join it. After becoming the tenth prisoner to join the second strike, McElwee became, on August 8 at 11.30am, the ninth to die. He had been on hunger strike for sixty-two days. His place was taken by IRA volunteer Patrick Sheehan. Sheehan was followed on August 17 by another IRA volunteer, Jackie McMullan.

By this time, INLA hunger striker Michael "Mickey" Devine was approaching the point of no return. Devine, from the Creggan area in Derry, had taken over from O'Hara as OC of INLA prisoners in the prison. Known as "Red Mickey", Devine was resolutely socialist, though the nickname had as much to do with the colour of his hair. He was born on May 26, 1954, on an American airbase just outside Derry. This airbase housed many Catholic families in very poor conditions; a result, said Nationalists, of their exclusion under a sectarian housing policy by Derry Corporation – which was run entirely by Protestants despite the city being eighty per cent Catholic.

In 1968, Devine, whose father died of leukaemia when he was eleven, witnessed the events of fifth October, when the RUC clamped down on a civil-rights demonstration that had included Protestants as well as Catholics. Devine later observed that "within a month, everyone had become a political activist".

By late 1969, after the situation in Derry had deteriorated, Devine joined others manning the barricades and becoming involved with the Young Socialists and the Labour Party. He also became a member of the James Connelly Republican Club, another indication of his socialist allegiance, and soon after joined the Derry Brigade of the left-wing Official IRA.

In 1972, Devine was on the anti-Internment march that ended with Bloody Sunday, fleeing with others from the shooting that ended with fourteen dead. The killings, and the Army's insistence that they fired at armed men only after they themselves had come under attack – an explanation later officially exposed as a lie – caused even such moderate nationalists as Hume of the SDLP to declare: "That's it. It's a United Ireland or nothing". For Devine, it was further confirmation of the injustice of British rule and the need, in his mind, for unflinching resistance.

In September that year, he returned home one day to find his mother dead in the house. Without warning, she had died as a result of a brain tumour. He married the following year, aged 19, and went on to have two children. In 1974, in common with most Official IRA volunteers in Derry he became disillusioned with the then ceasefire and "fireside Republican" approach of the increasingly un-militaristic Official IRA. He became a founder member of the INLA, which essentially represented those Officials who wanted to continue the "war".

Devine was arrested in September 1976 after an arms raid on an INLA weaponry in Co Donegal. Convicted and sentenced to twelve years in prison on June 29, 1977, he immediately joined the Blanketmen. Devine volunteered for the hunger strikes in 1981 and on August 20, at 7.50am, he died after fasting for sixty days.

Later that day, Carron won the by-election caused by Sands's death. He took more than 31,000 votes – half the total number of ballots cast. This represented an increased majority and, as Carron was not a hunger striker or even a prisoner himself, standing as a proxy anti-H-block candidate, it clearly demonstrated to Republicans the potential durability of electoral politics, even as a supplementary tactic. The SDLP had stood aside, which provided an indication of the polarisation between Nationalists and Unionists.

The election of Carron did not outwardly affect the way the British approached the crisis, however, which in their view was now coming to a slow and painful end. Thatcher refused to meet the newly elected MP to discuss the prisoners' situation. The same day Devine died and Carron was elected, Pat McGeown's family took him of hunger strike.

The bulk of the prisoners, to varying degrees, still wanted to keep going and new volunteers continued to come forward for the hunger strike. On August 24, IRA volunteer Bernard Fox joined the fast and on 31st August Hugh Carville, an IRA volunteer, joined the hunger strike. To some on the outside it seemed futile to carry on, but to many of the prisoners who had to endure conditions on the inside there was nothing to lose. It was felt among Republicans that by showing their commitment and determination, whatever the final outcome of the strike itself, the prisoners were not only asserting their political status and refusal to be criminalized, but their ongoing defiance would inspire radical political action among Nationalists in future. But the price being paid was a heavy one.

On September 4, the same day that Devlin was taken off hunger strike by his family after fasting for fifty-two days, there was a meeting of the National H-block committee in Dundalk. There, the INLA, conscious that they had only twenty-eight men left in the blocks and might soon run out of volunteers for hunger strike, announced that they would not be putting forward hunger strikers at the same rate as before.

There were still prisoners, however, willing to keep the pressure up. Three days later, after McKeown's family intervened to save his life when he lapsed into a coma following seventy days on hunger strike, Carville was joined on hunger strike by IRA man John Pickering. By now, however, the British government was counting on the initiative of Fr Faul and others to persuade the families to take the most critically ill prisoners off, effectively ending the crisis.

Realising that the strike was near to running its course, Republicans were aware that beyond the spectre of short-term defeat lay brighter prospects. It was noted in The Washington Post on September 12 that the IRA had made an increase in funds, inspired by sympathy for the hunger strikes. The organisation's ability to continue with the long war would remain, whatever the outcome of the hunger strikes, and far from being demoralised both the IRA and Sinn Fein found that they were also experiencing an upsurge in recruitment.

Moreover, the many non-Republican organisations who had supported the prisoners were a source of encouragement and ideas as to how the struggle could be progressed in political directions. Also on September 12, James Prior, considered to be a Tory "Wet", was appointed Secretary Of State for Northern Ireland. The outgoing incumbent, Atkins, was left feeling embittered after faithfully following what he believed was Thatcher's line during the strike.

Within days of being in Ireland, Prior went into the H-blocks and talked to Republicans. He also saw the remaining hunger strikers, but there was no negotiation with them. Nonetheless, it was a significant move as this was the first visit to the prison by a secretary of state for two years

There was a shifting of position on the hunger strikers' side, too, although those in the Thatcher government hoping for a rapid resolution would be disappointed. While September 14 saw Gerard Hodgins of the IRA join the strike, followed a week later by fellow IRA volunteer James Devine, September 24 brought Fox's hunger strike came to an end after thirty-two days due to medical complications. Two days after that, McCloskey came off hunger strike when his family had made it clear they would take him off as soon as he went into a coma. Despite the undoubted determination of the men still on hunger strike, there were now moves to bring it to an end.

On September 17, in a comm to Gerry Adams, McFarlane noted that he had been asked by some prisoners to consider coming off the hunger strike as they felt that their "present troubles might be insurmountable". That day Fr Faul, who had been described in a statement by prisoners the previous day as a "treacherous, conniving man", convened a meeting of five of the remaining six hunger-strike families and it was agreed, reluctantly in some cases, that it was time to end it.

On September 30, Prior gave a press conference urging the hunger strikers to "give up". He made a point, however, of refusing to talk in terms of victory or defeat. He considered such terms "counterproductive" given the sensitivities of the situation and, as he believed the momentum of events was going his way, he did not want to create new obstacles by challenging the prisoners with gratuitous triumphalism.

Events were moving towards a conclusion. On Saturday October 3, McFarlane was allowed to see the hunger strikers after suggesting that the strike could be ended. All were agreed that the hunger strike had run its course and, at 3.15pm, all remaining hunger strikers ended their fasts. The hunger strike was over.

The tragic dilemma that forced the protest to a conclusion – keep dying with little prospect of success, or stop now and throw away what they have suffered for – is remembered well by McKearney, one of the 1980 hunger strikers. He recalls:

> I don't believe the hunger strikes could have been sustained beyond the point it had reached in October 1981. This wasn't a Turkish prison hunger strike scenario. It wouldn't be never ending. The way it ended was a sort of drift. Father Faul effectively tidied up the loose ends. He came in for a lot of stick, but he couldn't have done it by himself. He couldn't have done it without the families wanting it to happen. He was basically responding to their desires and wishes. In a way it was a shame that it was left to him, and the families.
>
> It would have been much cleaner if the Army Council had called it off.

It was a hard, hard choice for them. They had not only to consider the men who'd died on hunger strike, but there were some 200 or so other volunteers who had died since the conflict began. There was that legacy as well. It was a terrible choice they'd have had to make. But that, in my subjective view, is what leadership is for. You make decisions. Some of them will inevitably be bad ones, but hopefully most of them will be good ones. But if you don't make decisions, then you won't make good ones, will you? So leadership must accept responsibility.

Johnny Donaghy, Republican activist, also recalls the period when it seemed the hunger strikers' opponents were not prepared to give ground, even after many men had lost their lives. There were pressures in the Republican and Nationalist communities brought to bear on the H-block campaign to call a halt to the hunger strikes.

We really thought that the government would give them something at the last minute, to avoid his [Bobby Sands's] dying. In fact, I think that it wasn't until after Joe McDonnell died that I realised that the Brits would just keep letting them die. It would have been around that time that some of our own supporters began approaching me and other H-block activists, asking us to speak to someone further up the chain and see if we could get it stopped. I felt so sorry for the families.

Donaghy believed the IRA leadership were in an impossible situation as the hunger strike drew to a close. Even if the Army Council had ordered the prisoners off he, like many Republicans, questions whether the command would have been heeded.

But would they have come off? After what these prisoners had been through, they were very determined. Sinn Fein were against the hunger strikes to begin with and it's doubtful anyone could have stopped it if they'd insisted. There were different schools of thought. Some thought the Brits would just let them die. Others didn't agree.

Within three days of the strikes being halted, Prior stated a number of concessions in public. The right of the prisoners to wear their own clothes was conceded and fifty per cent remission restored. There was also to be more free association, while parcel and visiting rights had already been agreed. Prison work, a major bone of contention to the prisoners, was abandoned after several incidents persuaded the authorities that due to the uncooperative approach of the prisoners safety and security could be compromised. As for political status, it was hard to argue that anything less had been achieved by the election victories of Sands, Agnew, Doherty and Carron.

Chapter Twelve:

The genie out of the bottle

Despite the loss of ten of their most committed comrades without a public concession on political status, allowing Thatcher to claim the IRA itself was defeated and still criminal, Republicans began to realise that the prison protests they had effectively begun in 1976 had actually borne some fruit. It had activated a potentially vast constituency of political support, locally and internationally. Behind the perceived triumphalism of the Thatcher government's public façade, moreover, it was now apparent to many in the British camp that they would have to give some ground.

Even as early as 1978, pressure had been growing on the British from figures in the Irish establishment; pressure the hunger strikes now made unavoidable. Although many Republicans still feel that the Catholic Church should have done more overall to aid their cause, Cardinal Ó Fiaich had become one of the very first high-profile figures to become interested in the prisoners' plight. Ó Fiaich had become instrumental in pushing British and Irish governments to address the prison issue when they were under no great general public pressure to do so.

While Ó Fiaich did not succeed in getting Thatcher to concede to the prisoners' demands, he did help concentrate the minds of Nationalist politicians in Ireland, particularly in Fianna Fail, as well as those of the clergy and other empathetic elements. As the political class in Ireland became more interested in the anti-H-block protest and the hunger strikes, even if many of them did so because they sensed a potential threat rather than out of real concern, that political class became more out of step with the UK government and parliament generally. While to Republicans it looked as though the Fianna Fail government in the south was doing nothing, Haughey was concerned that he'd have to pay an uncomfortable degree of lip service in support of compromise on the prisons issue, lip service that might somehow entrap him at some later stage.

Enormous tensions had built up as the crisis entered the summer of 1981. Some Fianna Fail members put pressure on Haughey, who was, they reminded him, the leader of "The Republican Party". Cynics have suggested that tensions arose between the two governments because Haughey wanted the British to adopt a position that would take him off the hook with his own grass roots. After the hunger strikes had ended in October of that year, Taoiseach Garret Fitzgerald of Fine Gael, who replaced Haughey at the southern Irish general election in June 1981, met Thatcher that November. Fitzgerald was distinctly anti-Republican and basically supportive of Thatcher's stand. So while there was no real conflict between these two leaders, there remained many in Ireland, including in the Irish establishment, that were bitter towards Britain for making their lives more difficult than they had to be and by displaying a callousness that was seen as anti-Irishness by some.

The hunger strike crisis damaged the Anglo-Irish relationship in that sense. However, both parties soon recognised some rapprochement was essential if their relationship was to work as well as it needed to. This was considered vital due to the shared security concerns of both countries along the north-south border. In July 2005, Fitzgerald recollected that he saw in the early 1980s the potential for northern Republicans to destabilise the southern government as well as the political life of Northern Ireland. While Thatcher had been tough on the hunger strikes, behind the scenes her government realised that some reassessments regarding the British view of Ireland and of moderate nationalism in the north; that is, the SDLP, were necessary. This development did not go unnoticed in Republican circles. In the depressed atmosphere of apparent defeat among Republicans in the aftermath of the hunger strikes, this was seen as a gleam of light several reasons.

Firstly, the tumults of the summer had created the situation whereby Britain, even under a seemingly victorious Thatcher, had to consider – if only privately – concessions to Irish nationalism. That was the advice from some in the British establishment to Thatcher, and from Fitzgerald. Others, such as close Thatcher confidant and conservative MP Ian Gow, who appeared to be Airey Neave's heir as Thatcher's security guru in Ireland, were wary and reluctantly supportive of such moves. The scale and determination of support for the hunger strikers in Ireland and from all over the world, whether justified or not, had taken the British by surprise – as did the scale of the fallout on the streets of Northern Ireland.

Although Thatcher was sure her government had won, and although many in the security forces were pleased Republicans had suffered a massive blow, there were many in government and intelligence circles who rapidly reached the conclusion that Britain couldn't afford to go through it all again. The price of another "victory" of this sort could be ruinous. Her apparent success ensured Thatcher could continue to call the IRA criminals. The trouble was less people in Ireland, and around the world, believed her now. The deaths of the ten men had showed the British that Republicanism as such couldn't be beaten and that helped sustain Republican morale through the years of "the long war". Maybe the IRA couldn't win – but neither could the British, not completely, and not in a manner that ensured the IRA would never return. That was an important consequence of the hunger strikes.

In that sense, the hunger strikes lent credence to the notion of "the long war". Republicans could endure more than the British thought. The sacrifice of the hunger strikes, moreover, invoked a historic Republican notion of victory in defeat. Terence MacSwiney, an IRA hero from the War of Independence and Sinn Fein Lord Mayor of Cork who died on hunger strike in 1920, had said: "It's not those who inflict the most who win, it's those who can endure the most." If a Republican defeat could be a victory, how could Republicans lose?

Secondly, in southern Irish and British circles it was thought prudent to become more familiar with current Republican thinking. Republicans, it was realised, could potentially become part of the body politic at some point in the future, however distant. This in turn must have encouraged those who scented the possibility of what would become known during the peace process as a "pan-Nationalist front". This would come to consist of Republicans, "constitutional" Nationalists in the north; i.e., the SDLP, as well as in the south – to say nothing of global support, particularly from powerful Irish-Americans. In addition, the Church, or some within it at least, considered that any communication which could end the cycle of violence and grief must be pursued. It would be wrong to say that the scent of a kind of grand coalition was that of an inevitability, as hindsight might suggest. Rather, it was a faint possibility.

In recalling this incipient development, it must be stressed that Republicans were still seen by many as pariahs. Nevertheless, some in the Church, in Fianna Fail, some in the SDLP, and some "rogue elements" in the southern establishment saw engagement with Republicans as not only inevitable, but essential to some sort of accommodation. The realisation of this fact was helped enormously by the latent Republican sentiment displayed by many ordinary people on both sides of the border during the hunger strikes. Many seemingly empathetic elements foresaw this as a source of competition, threat and eventual destabilisation as much as anything else.

It's fair to assume that Republicans always had their ears to the ground, as did the British. And Fianna Fail had some members more sympathetic to the movement than they cared to admit publicly. It was suggested during the research for this book that the British said things to the southern government, to Church figures and others knowing full well it would be passed down the line to the IRA. The beauty of this was they could always deny it was happening; it was never direct and always unmentionable. And if this is in fact what had occured the IRA leadership would have been alive to the possibility that it was being manipulated but, even allowing for that possibility, political contact of any description would have ultimately been something to build on.

Secret contacts, channels and go-betweens between the IRA and the British are public knowledge now. It has been revealed that the Tories from Major back to Thatcher were talking to Republicans for years, even though they denied it in the House of Commons. We also know about agent Oatley's contacts during the hunger strikes themselves, and previously. Despite the voluminous references to such contact, notably in Ed Moloney's *Secret history of the IRA*, and the journalism of David McKittrick and others, some contacts for this book have either suggested or in one case plainly stated that there is a lot more to be learned about communication between the British and the IRA.

It was immediately apparent to some in the southern and British establishments, for example, that the Republican constituency had come alive in the aftermath of the hunger strikes. There was a feeling that "someone somewhere had to engage with it or at least address some of its agenda". But those who had such foresight ended up being constricted for a decade by their own side's public position that Republicans were "murderers, Godfathers" and so on. One source states:

> A historic opportunity to start the peace process fully and comprehensively at that time was lost. The conditions were right. The British, Republicans, the Republic, all were exhausted – traumatised, even. If an olive branch had been offered at that time, which would have taken

real courage, then maybe we could have avoided a decade of conflict. Having said that, there is no doubt that the hunger strikes confronted many politicians with the reality that Republicans were not going to go away, as they say – and so they had to be engaged with politically. Predictably, even then, this was resisted, and every other conceivable alternative – like bolstering the SDLP – was explored. The reality was ignored; that the Republican genie was out the bottle.

After the hunger strikes, Sinn Fein had many eager new recruits; some from the H-block campaign, others newly radicalised Nationalists. There were not just political benefits. There were military ones, too. The IRA had a whole new generation of recruits. The standing of Republicanism went through the roof in many Nationalist areas. Toleration and active support for IRA activities grew. While the battle for the five demands appeared to have been lost, the battle for the hearts and minds of Nationalist Ireland – especially in the six-counties/Northern Ireland – was on the way to being won.

Such benefits were for Republicans, not for the British soldiers, prison officers, RUC members and – all too often – innocent civilians who were in the front line of the resurgent conflict. It was clear that whatever political thought processes had been stimulated by reaction to the hunger strikes, armed struggle would not play second fiddle to it. In fact, at the Sinn Fein Ard Fheis (annual conference) in Dublin in November 1981, Danny Morrison, the prominent Republican and then editor of *An Phoblacht*, addressed the internally contentious issue of taking part in elections by making his now famous speech, in which he said: "Who here really believes we can win the war through the ballot box? But will anyone here object if, with a ballot paper in one hand and the Armalite in the other, we take power in Ireland?"

While many Republicans have since denied that Morrison was espousing official policy, the phrase stuck as it seemed to many Republicans and others to epitomise the notion that both armed and electoral battles had a part to play in the Irish Republican struggle. Morrison has subsequently stated that the phrase simply came to him as he approached the podium to speak. And Martin McGuinness later said it was the first time he had ever heard the phrase. Others have commented that Sinn Fein leaders on the executive committee sitting behind Morrison as he spoke were "flabbergasted", one of them being said to be concerned that "we were making policy on the hoof". Whether official policy or not, the phrase became one of the most memorable of the Troubles.

Chapter Thirteen:

'Then everything kicked off'

In the new political climate, Republican armed struggle was reassessed but by no means replaced. Far from fostering greater understanding between divided communities, moreover, the hunger strikes' most immediate effect on the streets of Northern Ireland was to unleash a fresh round of conflict. Others caught up in the Troubles, such as British Army and RUC personnel, have their own memories and perspectives of what they faced on the ground at time. Needless to say, these are generally very different to those of Republicans. Yet, amid the anger and bitterness at the fact they were now more than ever the "bad guys" in the eyes of Nationalists while the hunger strikers and the IRA were presented as martyrs, there is a grudging recognition that some things had changed for the better as a result of the hunger strikes.

"Harry" was a British Army soldier who did several tours of Northern Ireland over many years. He remembers things from a British military perspective, recalling:

> In the early days, I didn't think of the IRA, or the Protestants for that matter, as terrorists. That seemed to come a year or so later. The RUC thought differently and, as time went on, we came to share their view in the main. We were brought to that view by the constant rioting in some areas, although that was carried out mainly by civilians and hooligans. During the worst violence, of the early 70s, it was easy to portray – and to think of – the IRA as terrorists, because they committed appalling acts of terror. Even in their own communities, people were sickened by some of their actions.
>
> Events like Bloody Sunday were a good way of measuring their status

on the ground, their "street cred" if you like. This was important to us because if their community standing was high, then we could not trust our intelligence 100 per cent. Nor could we get close enough often enough to gather our own high-grade intelligence when the IRA was well thought of. It did seem to fluctuate from one week to the next in some areas.

After Bloody Sunday, for example, all hell broke loose. I remember some of my colleagues being very pissed off about what happened on Bloody Sunday (a) because it was clear from day one our lads had killed innocent civilians and (b) because the IRA were instantly heroes, which we knew not to be true, who had more recruits than they could use. In my view, Bloody Sunday created an enemy army overnight. The aftermath seemed to last for years. Then we got things under some kind of control. I remember that awful expression "acceptable level of violence". It did seem that while not over, the Troubles, as I had known them, were not dominating every day life for ordinary Irish people of either religion. We thought they'd [the IRA] shot their bolt. I was feeling hopeful – not easy to do when you've seen what I have. And there were still terrible, terrible times. But it felt like the beginning of the end. Then a period of sort of stalemate, if you like. Still, if not going forwards, at least we were not going backwards.

But then came the hunger strikes. And then everything kicked off. It was just like Bloody Sunday all over again. Overnight, the IRA were the "good guys" again. Our intelligence became far weaker as people are less inclined to grass on "heroes". Even some informants have a conscience and periodically feed you as little as they think they can get away with feeding you. It still functioned, of course; not all agents were politically motivated, I'm pleased to say. And the best agents are generally not really affected by the political climate as such, as they have their own motivations anyway.

There was a new viciousness. Once again, a whole generation of volunteers joined the IRA's ranks, only this time they were joining forces with a generation of seasoned hard men, experienced terrorists who knew the ropes. I found the whole thing utterly depressing. It was the first moment that I found myself believing that this really would go on forever. It was hopeless. Add to that the difficulty of portraying men willing to lay down their lives for principle as terrorists, and you can appreciate that the "hearts and minds" game was well and truly a bogey. The hunger strikes forced many to re-examine their attitudes to the Irish, and to the Provisional IRA community in particular, myself included. Not that I became defeatist. Just more resigned to what had to be done.

Harry is nevertheless reluctant to concede that the British Army had any kind of sneaking regard for "people prepared to lay down their lives for their principles".

The hunger strikers weren't the only ones to do so. My men were prepared to do it every day they walked the streets; as were the RUC, the UDR and others. Where are their murals? Republicans might think my men and I were wrong to be where we were in 1981. But they could not and should not have doubted our courage. I'm trying to turn your argument around a bit. Respect should be a two-way street. But as you know, it isn't. And the hunger strikers had choices that the PIRA didn't allow others. People forget that during that dreadful summer and beyond, it was not just the hunger strikers who died. I often think of the relatives of others who were murdered by the IRA during that time. There are no murals made in their honour. I have no "sneaking regard" whatsoever.

However, I will say this. The fact that these men were prepared to do what they did made an impression on me. I find the canonisation and martyring of them revolting, frankly. But the difference between Bloody Sunday and the hunger strikes is that something appears to have been built on the ashes of the hunger strikes. I don't pretend to like it. But a political Sinn Fein is marginally easier to accept, if one considers the alternative is a murderous Sinn Fein/IRA. It seems to me that Republicans found a political voice in the wake of the hunger strikes. It does not fill my heart with joy. It just makes me feel a little bit less hopeless. One day, maybe I'll see some of them as soldiers. They had brave men among them. The hunger strikes demonstrated that irrefutably. But, so did I. So don't expect me to honour their dead when I know they won't honour ours.

Members of the RUC also felt they were under a new wave of attack in the immediate aftermath of the hunger strikes. In 1981, "Donald" was a 24-year-old RUC member. He had joined not out of any sense of Protestant duty, but out of a sense of community and a belief in law and order. Despite all his training, the peculiar context of being a policeman in Northern Ireland conjured up many questions in his mind.

Until the hunger strikes and everything that went with it, I was looking after the community, no matter what their religion. If someone called me to help them, if their house had been burgled, or if they'd been beaten up or whatever, do you think I would have had the faintest interest in their religion? Of course not. Now, that's not to ignore that there were bigots in the police. This is Northern Ireland after all. There are bigots in every occupation. And people were bigoted against us too. But most of RUC officers I knew would have helped anyone. On duty they were professionals. To say the whole force went around picking fights with Catholics, or hating them is nonsense.

Now, some who'd been there longer than me would have had a frame of mind that was different to mine and ones my age. They were fighting "the enemy" which was terrorism. To me that attitude seemed alien to the job we were being asked to do. We weren't an army. I did not join to "defend Ulster"; I joined to defend society, law and order. At that time I would not have rushed into the streets to protest if we'd been taken into a United Ireland in a democratic way. But after the hunger strikes, I understood the attitude of these older cops better. I'd led a sheltered existence in the police up to that point. But during and immediately after the hunger strikes, the attitude of people to us changed. It did feel as if we were under attack. Now I understood that I was at war. Whether it would have happened anyway, or not, I don't know. All I know is that it changed the way I looked at my work.

The hunger strikes and their aftermath also changed the way officers like Donald looked at some IRA volunteers and their supporters. There was an understanding that, while the RUC were still at war against an often brutal enemy that had to be defeat, that enemy contained human beings who could not easily be demonised.

Look, let's be honest. Some people will just hate other people and that's that. I couldn't care less if you're a Buddhist or whatever. But if you break the law, that's your problem. The only thing about the hunger strikers is that criminals don't starve themselves to death. I know of

IRA men that done pure terrorism, real brutal killings, mutilations and torture. But them ones that starved themselves were different. It showed me, anyway, that not all "the terrorists" were scum.

But now I understood we were in a war and at times that did make me want to take the battle to the other side. By the other side, I don't mean Catholics; I mean law-breakers, terrorists, freedom fighters, call them what you want.

Nowadays, I'm a DUP man myself. I think it's better that the IRA goes for politics now. Things are better now. I don't know about power-sharing. I'm not being anti-Catholic at all, just anti-IRA. They are still the enemy. But I'd rather fight them in elections than anywhere else. They have a mandate. We have to be big enough to live with that. And if it's the price of peace, well, I'll think about it. It's not easy. The ones that shout about the IRA done this and done that – they are very brave in a politician's suit. They don't need to tell me what the IRA done. They didn't fight the IRA – I did. And I'd do it again if I had to, do it again in a minute. But I hope I don't have to.

Another RUC member from that era is "Colin", who joined the force in 1973. As with Donald, Colin joined the RUC to help people and to try and do some good. He'd wanted to be a "bobby" the way people in other less controversial circumstances might want to be a policeman, or a fireman, or whatever. In various conversations with the author, he has expressed a profound abhorrence of bigotry of any description and would not recognise the profile of the RUC suggested by Republicans.

I was one of the police motorcycle riders who escorted some of the coffins of the hunger strikers from the prison to their family homes. Irrespective of how and why the men died, or who they were, I saw it as my job, my responsibility, to get their remains back home to their loved ones without incident or whatever. I saw it as my duty to protect the remains from abuse as they went through areas where maybe the people didn't agree with them.

I felt sorry for the men in the coffins because I think their organisa-tion thought they were worth more to their cause dead than alive. I think they were put up to it by the IRA and that the Provos wanted the propaganda out of it. I formed this view because this is what we would have heard through people like Special Branch, and they would know because they had informants in the IRA. See, that's why the IRA have sought so hard to discredit the Special Branch, because they were so effective at infiltrating the IRA.

There's no doubt that the Nationalist population were radicalised against us in our normal policing role. We were just doing a job after all. I wasn't against anybody. In fact, when I was growing up I saw one night on the TV how Catholics were complaining that the RUC was bigoted. I said to my father who was watching with me: "Well, I wasn't brought up to be a bigot, so I'll join the RUC and show them that it's not bigoted." I joined in 1973. With the odd exception, I did not know bigots in the RUC. In fact, a man around at that time was a Catholic from the Short Strand who went on to become a Chief Superintendent.

One effect of the hunger strikes was that the IRA and everyone else now knew that Thatcher would not give in one little bit. Also, the new environment was a breeding ground for more IRA volunteers and supporters. See, at that point, the IRA was really finished but the whole hunger strike thing enabled them to keep on for another decade or so.

In hindsight, the government would have been better dealing with the hunger strikes by making more use of the fact that the hunger strikers themselves did not want to die and that they were being forced into it. That might have brought about the end of it sooner.

When asked whether he has any reflections on the fact that many of the Republicans committed to the peace process and instrumental to the cease-fires, the Belfast Agreement and decommissioning are former Blanketmen, IRA prisoners and former hunger strikers, Colin's response is telling. Some might say many influential Republicans from the hunger-strike era have played a huge part in ensuring "the war is over". Colin sees things differently:

But it's not over. The war's still going on. They are just fighting it with different means.

Another security service in the front line was the UDR. A former UDR intelligence officer offers a considered reflection on the hunger strikes that he and his colleagues had known was on the cards from their information-gathering. He recalls he and his colleagues failed to anticipate the determination of the prisoners this time around. He also considers how the events of 1981 changed the way the UDR thought about the enemy, how the enemy itself adapted, and makes plain who he believes were the real winners and losers of the hunger-strike campaign.

> In early 1981, we knew IRA prisoners had laid plans for another hunger strike to be led by Bobby Sands. However, intelligence-gathering failed to indicate this time it would be all or nothing as far as Republicans were concerned; that there would be no compromise.
>
> Initially, within the intelligence network there was a feeling of déjà vu about the hunger strike: we had been here before and seen it all. Few thought it would end in death. There was a general belief the IRA would take things to the brink once again before another compromise deal was struck. However, subsequent events were to prove us all wrong.
>
> Five days into Sands's hunger strike, the independent MP for Fermanagh-South Tyrone, Frank Maguire, died. Almost immediately intelligence showed Republicans wanted Sands to run as a candidate in the by-election. It was an astute political move and Sands, the H-block candidate, was elected to the consternation of British politicians and military commanders. Furthermore, his election opened up a new road of political opportunities for the Republican movement. Looking back it also put Sinn Fein on a par with the IRA. Crucially, at that time the British failed to recognise Republicans had tapped into a previously un-used well of political support. That same political support would prove to be the sustaining source of the next stage in the 'Brits out of Ireland' battle.
>
> Although Sands was a Republican and the IRA had killed members of my regiment, there was a grudging admiration inside me for the cour-age he had shown during his hunger strike – but there was no sympathy for his cause. However, that's as far as it went and there was no way I would ever consider expressing those comments within military cir-cles. As far as I was concerned the IRA was still the enemy. Despite the ongoing hunger strike there was no let up in the IRA Provisional Army Council's operations against the security forces. In the seven months of the hunger strike the Provos killed five UDR soldiers. It was business as usual as far as the Provisionals were concerned.
>
> As the hunger strike continued and more IRA died, it became clear neither side was prepared to give in. Intelligence sources showed

Republican prisoners were still committed to the cause. We wondered how many more would die before the impasse was broken. In all ten men died before the hunger strike finally collapsed. It officially ended on October 3, 1981.

What did it achieve? Initially nothing as the end was seen as a victory for the British Government. However, now I don't believe that to be the case. I think, ultimately, the IRA were the victors as within a short time Republican prisoners got everything they wanted. Sometimes, when I look back at the events of 1981 I ask myself the question: "Would it have not been simpler if the authorities had given the prisoners what they wanted?" I think the answer is "yes", accommodation not confrontation and all that ...

Over the years the hunger strikes have become legendary. Those who died have become martyrs for the Irish Republican cause. Did Bobby Sands and his nine fellow prisoners die in vain? I think not, as their deaths were the catalyst that exploded Sinn Fein onto the world wide political stage. Within two decades, Sinn Fein has emerged from the political wilderness to evolve into a sophisticated political force in modern day Irish politics. That is the real legacy of the hunger strikes of 1981.

Those members of the security services who were perhaps the most personally engaged with Republicans on a day-to-day basis during 1981 were prison officers. Their proximity to the front line offered some of them relatively intimate portraits of the hunger strikers. "Albert" retired from the Northern Ireland Prison Service in 2001. During his employment with the prison authorities, he served in the Crumlin Road and Maze/Long Kesh prisons. He came into contact with some of Northern Ireland's most notorious paramilitaries – Loyalist and Republican. However, as far as Albert was concerned, the IRA hunger strikes were the most significant event he experienced. He recalls the Maze/Long Kesh prison was awash with rumour and speculation in the days preceding the IRA hunger strike. He claims prison authorities were aware the IRA was considering using the hunger-strike tactic but believed the IRA lacked the willpower to see it through.

It was a serious miscalculation by the prison staff and the British of the IRA, and the dedication of IRA men to die for the cause. When the IRA prisoners went on hunger strike the majority of prison staff thought it would be over within days. Either the IRA or the British government would give in and call it a day, but that didn't happen. At that stage the atmosphere changed and we knew these men would fast to the death. Meals were still supplied to all prisoners on the H-blocks irrespective of whether or not they were refusing to take food. I was on the same H-block as Bobby Sands and, as the strike progressed, I must admit I grew to respect him. Not because he was in the IRA or anything like that. I respected him as a human being. A man who was so committed to what he believed in that he was prepared to die for it. It was amazing.

Despite what anyone says about the IRA, there was a dignity about those men. They were all emaciated, some of them were almost blind, but they were dignified at all times. It was as if they had resigned them-selves to death and were prepared for it when it came. I think it's fair to say the majority of prison officers that served in the Maze at that time would grudgingly admit to having some respect for the IRA men who starved to death in the early 1980s. Personally, it left a lasting im-pression on me. However, I have to say that in the years that followed the majority of IRA men I came into contact with through the prison system did not have the same ideals or commitment that Bobby Sands or Francis Hughes had in 1981. A lot of the old Republicanism died with Sands and Hughes, and a new breed of IRA men evolved as a direct result of the hunger strikes.

Another voice from the prison staff is "Tommy", who retired from the service in 2004. He had given more than thirty years of service and attained the rank of governor when he decided to call it a day. Those three decades clearly took their toll on him both physically and mentally. He exhibits all the classic symptoms of combat fatigue. Tommy is in his mid-fifties but looks a lot older. He is decidedly war-weary.

During his time with the Prison Service, Tommy served in all three Northern Ireland's jails – the Maze, or Long Kesh as it was originally known, Crumlin Road and Maghaberry. He has literally experienced it all – Internment, the compounds, the dirty protests, Loyalist and Republican hunger strikes, and the murder of LVF leader Billy Wright.

Once fiercely loyal to his chosen vocation, Tommy is now somewhat cynical about the prison service and its political paymasters in the Northern Ireland Office. The staunch loyalty of the early days, when Tommy believed the system could do no wrong, has long since been eroded. It has been replaced by a candid recognition that Northern Ireland's unique penal system was politically manipulated by terrorists and governments alike.

> We were the filling in a political sandwich. On one side was the NIO with its political advisors and securicrats. On the other were the paramilitaries with their intimidation and threats of violence. In between was us, the prison staff, and over the years we were rendered impotent by the authorities themselves. I don't care what anyone says, politics dictated the running of the prisons – particularly the Maze and Crumlin Road. No matter what was said it was never going to be any different, politics is a way of life in Northern Ireland irrespective of what side of the prison walls you are on.

Tommy claims he first became disillusioned with the Northern Ireland prison system at the time of the 1981 Republican hunger strike. He says the strike completely changed his attitude to prison management and prisoners alike.

> 'I was promoted to Senior Officer rank several months before the first hunger strike began in October 1980. The idea was nothing new as far as prison staff was concerned. The IRA had discussed using it as a tactic in the summer 1979, but it didn't materialise then as the Republican leadership believed it would not generate sufficient support to keep it going. At that stage there was a feeling that the IRA had a bigger agenda in place than what was happening inside the Maze. At that time, I was working on H block 3 and we knew Brendan Hughes had asked for volunteers to go on hunger strike. In the end, the prisoners did their own thing and the IRA leadership had no option but to go along with the idea.
>
> Looking back now, I believe the 1981 hunger strike could have been averted had the Prison Authorities been prepared to try and work with the prisoners on what had been agreed at that time the first strike ended. I also think the British authorities could and should have encouraged prison management at the Maze more than they did. I was there at the time, and prison officers knew the 1981 hunger strike would never have happened if an agreement had been achieved between both parties. In my opinion, prison authority intransigence precipitated the second hunger strike and the death of ten Republican prisoners.

According to Tommy, there was a two-way flow of information between the intelligence services and senior prison management at the Maze/Long Kesh throughout the duration of the 1981 hunger strike. He recalls Prison officials were anxious to assess the mood within the Republican H-blocks, what the grass-roots feeling was. That information was in turn relayed onto the intelligence services and eventually to the Prime Minister.

We all knew the spooks had people inside the Maze and they were being briefed first hand by prison management. They were constantly monitoring the atmosphere within the Maze. It was difficult enough for us to carry on as normal at that time without having to act as intelligence gatherers as well. I remember when Bobby Sands died on 5th May 1981, emotions were running high inside the Maze. We had been told there were growing tensions between the IRA and the prisoners. We understood that the IRA Army Council had told the prisoners if any hunger striker died they were not to be replaced. As the officers in charge of the day-to-day running of a Republican H-block, we were told to watch out for any signs of internal divisions or lack of resolve on the Republican wings. But instead of shaking their resolve, Sands's death simply strengthened them and made them more determined to see it through to the end.

We also believed the British authorities wanted to settle the dispute and prevent any further loss of life. We knew there was some political initiative under way and were watching that with interest, as any agreement which met the prisoners' five demands would most certainly impact upon the role of the rank-and-file prison staff that had to implement it. Things were difficult enough at the Maze without some facing-saving deal that would get the British off the hook being foisted upon us.

I know now that a series of coded telephone calls took place between the government and the IRA throughout the hunger strike. At the time prison staff knew nothing about these calls, but they failed to broker any deal. However, it typified the way ordinary prison staff were kept in the dark about any developments within the Maze during the first half of 1981. I don't think either the prison authorities or the NIO had much thought for prison staff at that time. They wanted the hunger strike to end and the views of the men at the coalface counted for very little indeed'.

Tommy believes the IRA was as much to blame for the continuation of the 1981 hunger strike as the British government. A conversation he had some years later with one particular senior Republican prisoner provided him with what he claims was a revealing perspective of the IRA position in mid-1981. Here is Tommy's account of that meeting:

> He told me that by the time six men had died in 1981, the IRA leadership realised that they could maximise the propaganda available to them from the hunger strike. They [the IRA] weren't going to do anything that would stop the strike or impede the propaganda machine.
>
> The leadership, though, hoped in a way that there was a chance that the prisoners would call it off themselves – and the Army Council would have supported that 100 per cent. However, he [the senior Republican prisoner] said he believed the IRA leadership were failing to recognise exactly how the prisoners felt at the time. He told me that after years on the dirty protest and the degrading treatment meted out to them there was sheer determination to see it through. There was a comradeship between the IRA prisoners that had been built and strengthened by all they had gone through.
>
> I'll never forget his words that day. He said: "As far as we were concerned at that point in time, it was all or nothing. The fact that six of our comrades had already died on hunger strike made us even more determined than ever. The leadership never knew what that meant as they never experienced it the same way."

It should be underlined here that while the IRA leadership came over time to realise the propaganda value of the hunger strike, the prisoners themselves demonstrated a rock-solid commitment to continuing the protest until their five demands were met. IRA leaders themselves realised the prisoners would resist any attempt to take them off without those demands being conceded. As it became apparent that there was indeed a propaganda harvest to be had, utilising it in furtherance of the prisoners' cause made obvious sense to Republicans. It made sense, above all, to the prisoners themselves. They, after all, were the people who were forced to endure the conditions and protests in the H-blocks. Indeed, some prisoners felt that because the outside leadership did not have to go through day-to-day life on protest, year after year, it did not have the moral authority to call the shots.

The IRA leadership was well aware of this, having been told so in no uncertain terms by the prisoners. Overruling this strength of feeling could have been divisive and demoralising for Republicans, particularly for the prisoners. As we know, Gerry Adams did go into the jail in late July 1981 to lay out in the most stark terms what the options were. And when asked by the hunger striker Kieran Doherty how Kevin Lynch was, Adams replied: "You'll both be dead. I can go out there and announce that it's over." Doherty's reply summed up the hunger striker's mood: "Thatcher can't break us. I am not a criminal."

The view that the IRA leadership didn't understand that it was "all or nothing" carries little currency among Republicans. If they weren't sure before Sands died, nobody would have had any doubt after that. In fact, most Republicans would say that after the 1980 hunger strike was ended by British duplicity (according to both British and Republican sources), nobody involved on the Republican side would have doubted the prisoners' resolve.

Tommy's interpretation of the Republican position may be disputed, but his honestly expressed views cast valuable light on the thinking of men who had to endure life on the British state's front line for so many years. By the time the hunger strike was eventually called off in October 1981, Tommy admits he had developed a grudging admiration for those Republicans who were prepared to, and did, sacrifice everything. He recalls:

> When the hunger strike began at the Maze, it started off as a fight for political status. But it eventually developed into a much larger battle, which involved the complete Republican movement. The prisoners quickly realised that if they lost that battle they would eventually lose the whole war and all they stood for. Every bit of progress they had fought and died for would have stood for nothing. Quite simply, they had to hold out. Privately, I admire them for that. Publicly, even now, I would be ridiculed and vilified if I said that within my own circles.
>
> In October 1981 I was relieved the hunger strike was over. But looking back at it now in hindsight it has become a watershed for the IRA and the wider Republican family. After the deaths of ten men the British authorities realised they were fighting a ruthless enemy who was determined to keep going to the bitter end, irrespective of the cost. Sadly, neither the British government nor the prison service was able to draw on the lesson learned in 1981. Despite everything that happened

that year, they still stuck to the same old tactics and that helped pro-long the conflict here for another fifteen years or more.

When asked to sum up what the 1981 IRA hunger strike did for Republicans, Tommy's response is clear and candid:

A magnificent victory, one that propelled Republicans into the political arena.

Chapter Fourteen:

Loyalists take note

The security services and the British government were not, of course, the only agencies that had to devise ways of combating the hunger strikes and the organisation behind them. The Unionist community also provided a recruitment reservoir for Loyalist paramilitary organisations violently opposed to the aims of Republicans and determined to "keep Ulster British". The personal reflections here offer an insight into how the hunger strikes impacted on militant Unionists, their sense of purpose, their methods – which came to include collusion with the British security forces – and their understanding of the "enemy". Some of their reactions might be unexpected, surprising even. These reflections suggest a complex and diverse community.

"David" joined a paramilitary organisation in 1975. The organisation he joined was the UDA. Like RUC officer "Donald", David initially wanted to protect his "people". He perceived that Protestant rights were being eroded and that the Protestant state of Northern Ireland was being attacked by an illegal organisation that the Police couldn't defeat.

> The RUC knew who was doing what. We knew it, too. But they had to worry about rights and stuff like that. Now, I'm for law and order an all but when your enemy is using the law to take away your way of life, you have to use your own judgement. You have to suspend the normal rules. During wartime, different rules apply, don't they? Now, a prime minister had some years previously declared war on the IRA [Chichester-Clark, Northern Ireland Prime Minister after O'Neil and until March 1971]. That legitimised the UDA in my mind. My friends were in it. People who'd never done anything to anyone were in it. At that time the UDA was a legal organisation. So it was the most natural thing in the world to join.

I didn't really hate Catholics. There was the usual banter among us, but I wasn't a Fenian-hater like some of the lads, like the "Shankill Butchers". People bantered about that, too, even though deep down you knew it was wrong. But walking about condemning the murder of Catholics would have been seen as a sign of weakness. Besides, what about what they were doing to us? The IRA used to say that it wasn't sectarian. But that was bollocks. '75/'76 was not a time to show weakness. But you never believed anyone you knew would actually do things like that to people, unless they were IRA. That was different. We'd had Bloody Friday and loads of things like that there. Some of the lads wanted to take it out on any Catholic. But most fellas just wanted to hit the Provies or their supporters.

The Provies were a different breed in prison. When I was in jail it was like in the war films when the Gerry guard says: "For you, Tommy, the war is over." Maybe others felt different. I know that years later that changed. I'd done my bit and I wasn't alone in thinking about it like that. I was a wee bit jealous of some of them Provies in a way. When you caught the odd glimpse of them, I got the notion that they were in it for the rest of their lives. That might be me thinking about it years later on, but they were motivated compared to me. They knew what they were about. It didn't surprise me when they went on hunger strike, not a bit. If anything, it surprised me that it had taken so long 'cause you always heard they were talking about it.

Jail was my first real contact with them. I struck me that they were just fellas, like me. But, like I say, different. It was like they had a different agenda. Sometimes you'd be personable to them. And they'd be fine back. Sometimes you could even have a bit of banter with them. I looked into hunger striking, about what happens when your body goes without food. It didn't sound too healthy, to tell you the truth. So later, when I heard what these boys were going through, part of me said, "well, no one forced you". But part of me thought, I couldn't do that.

Don't get me wrong. I'm no fan. And I've seen what the IRA do. I hear this shite about 'bad jobs' [in relation to civilian casualties]. If the British Army put a foot wrong, the Provies want them hung for it. But when they fuck up, it's just a "bad job", no harm done. No inquiry, no court marshall. But now and again, more than twenty-four years later, I wonder how they [the hunger strikers] did it. How they went through it. How their families went through it. Did it change me? I really don't

know. It taught us all that if you were going to get involved, you'd better be serious. It made the IRA some new friends in America, I think.
That seemed to matter to them when it came to the ceasefires didn't it?
Can't say I followed it all that keenly. Did it change me? I suppose it'd
make you think, never underestimate your enemy.

David has not been involved with politics or paramilitarism since the
mid-1980s. His "war" was about hitting back. The hunger strikes brought
him to the realisation that it would take a more ruthless sort than him
to defeat the IRA. His story is not untypical of Loyalists of the period.
Others shared this realisation. It wasn't long, however, before a new breed
of Loyalist paramilitary gained the ascendancy within the UDA/UFF. By
the end of the decade, young Loyalist Leaders like Johnny Adair in the
UFF and Billy Wright in the UVF were part of ruthless organisations
whose killing rate matched that of the IRA. As well as Catholics unin-
volved in paramilitarism, these Young Turks targeted Sinn Fein members,
their families and IRA volunteers. This was a deliberate policy of either hitting IRA men or "their nearest and dearest", to quote one Loyalist source.
Some would say that this policy was a British government-sanctioned
policy with a name – collusion. There is ample evidence in the public
domain to demonstrate that this policy was not only conceived of by the
British security services, but managed by them on an almost "contracted
out" basis, as Loyalist killers were directed to people targeted by the FRU,
MI5 and others.

Some would contend that British/Loyalist collusion was an attack not
merely on the IRA, but perhaps more on the Republican movement's political arm, Sinn Fein. The party was becoming an embedded feature of
the political landscape, due in no small way to the hunger strikes and the
support for Sinn Fein that built up in their wake. To some, it seemed that
this newly efficient assault by Loyalists was on the entire Republican support base. Indeed, Metropolitan Police Commissioner Sir John Stevens's
investigation into collusion has shown that it was not carried out by a few
rotten apples, but was widespread. Several Loyalist operatives, it is alleged,
were not arrested as many of them were informers for the security services.
Arresting them, or even blowing their cover, would inhibit the authorities'
efforts against the IRA.

Neil MacKay, an Antrim-born, award-winning journalist working for Scotland's *Sunday Herald* newspaper, has investigated the Force

Reconnaissance Unit (FRU) and reported that not only did this British Army unit have informers in the Loyalist UDA and the UVF, but that the FRU actually directed the Loyalists' efforts, providing them with targets, escape routes and much protection from the law. Another source for this book has claimed that this was a policy approved "at the highest level" in the late days of the Thatcher administration. Some would say such approval had been intermittently given throughout the Troubles. This sets the scene for some of the contributions from Loyalists from later in the Troubles, from the late-1980s onwards. Many of these men believed they were doing the security forces' job for them. That some of these paramilitaries worked closely on occasion with military intelligence would only have enhanced that view.

Unsurprisingly, many Loyalists were, and indeed to a degree still are, reluctant to give any public recognition to the determination and dedication of IRA and INLA hunger strikers who died for a cause whose sole objective was the removal of a British presence in Ireland. To many Loyalists, the IRA will forever be the enemy. There was no sympathy whatsoever for IRA or INLA men who starved themselves to death on hunger strike. As far as Loyalists were concerned, it was a case of: "So what, it's no better than the IRA deserved." Few Loyalists interviewed for this book shared the sentiments expressed by "David".

"Keith" is a fifty-year-old Loyalist from Co Armagh. He was a member of the Ulster Volunteer Force at the time of the IRA hunger strike. In 1978, Keith's uncle, a part-time soldier in the Ulster Defence Regiment was shot dead by IRA gunmen as he returned from work. Although he severed all connection with the UVF a number of years ago, he still considers himself to be a "Loyalist". He describes the IRA as "murderous bastards". He believes Republicans have deliberately exploited the deaths of the hunger strikers, and that a myth has been deliberately created which portrays them as Irish patriots who willingly gave their lives in the cause of Irish Freedom. Keith's views may be considered extreme by some, offensive even, but they are shared by a number of Loyalists and others who perceive their communities to have suffered in the IRA's war against British rule.

> At the time of the hunger strikes, I was active in the UVF in mid-Ulster. That's where the war against the IRA was really fought. Not in Belfast as city men claimed – but here in mid-Ulster. Personally, I was glad to see every one of them starve to death. I only wish there had

been more of them. As far as I am concerned, they aren't Republican martyrs. They are dead IRA men – full stop.

These men took it upon themselves to die. But I believe they thought the Thatcher government would give in to their demands. As far as I am concerned, the hunger strikes backfired on the men involved. That's a positive thing as far as I am concerned. They got what they deserved. People forget the IRA men who went on the hunger strike had killed RUC men, UDR soldiers and innocent Protestants. They aren't martyrs.

Contrastingly, LVF leader Billy Wright had a different perspective on the effect of the hunger strike and those who took part in it. According to one source for this book who knew Wright well, Wright, although fiercely committed to the Unionist/Loyalist cause, differed from many rank-and-file Loyalists in that he had the capacity to analyse the effect the hunger strike would have on the IRA's military campaign. Wright recognised the dedication and strength of mind needed to commit to what was a self-imposed death sentence. While still in his early twenties the hunger strike left an impression on Wright, an impression that was to remain with him for the rest of his life. He realised that the Republican mindset differed drastically from that of the Loyalist, concluding that very few Loyalists would have the commitment to undertake a hunger-strike for their own cause. To Wright, the hunger strike was history in the making, as the following well-known quote attributed to him attests:

> I knew here was an organisation that was prepared to inflict so much pain and self-imposed torture upon itself. If it was prepared to do that for the sake of its own ideology, then what was it not prepared to do to other human beings who opposed its Republican objectives? What we were experiencing at that time was pure history. I knew then that Republicanism and the IRA had to be resisted.
>
> Republicans were prepared to do whatever it took to have their own way. If that meant starving to death, then so be it. I came across very few Loyalists who were prepared to die for their particular cause. The impact of the hunger strike was enormous. The sight of men starving themselves to death in the fight for Irish freedom impacted around the world. It was a massive PR victory for the IRA over the Thatcher government. Although IRA men died as a result of the hunger strike, their deaths brought many more young men into the Republican movement.

IRA recruitment soared as a direct result of the death of Bobby Sands and his fellow prisoners. The IRA subsequently analysed the impact of the hunger strike and built on the lessons they learned from it.

Wright's perceptive analysis in light of what Republicans had sacrificed for the hunger strikes casts valuable light on the thinking of hard-line Loyalist militants. However, while the impact of the hunger strikes on some people was to harden hatreds and deepen trenches, it is important to recognise that the historic events of 1980-1 did refract through the prism of the Unionist community at remarkably different angles. The recollections of former Orangeman and RUC reservist, Billy Leonard, provide a dramatic counterpoint to the reaction among Loyalist paramilitaries.

A Protestant from a Unionist background, and former SDLP member, Leonard is now a Sinn Fein councillor in Co Derry. He is a former member of the District Policing Partnership (DPP). Since Sinn Fein does not recognise the authority of such bodies, Leonard resigned when he switched his allegiance from the SDLP to Sinn Fein in 2004. He has been the subject of Loyalist death threats and his home has been attacked. Having studied the issue of the hunger strikes carefully, Leonard has first-hand experience of how such events played in the Unionist community at the time. He recalls:

> The era of the hunger strikes was a very important time for me, but from a perspective that was obviously different from my present-day colleagues. I was an outsider. However, I was still the young man who loved history and politics and had, by 1981, gone through four to five years of questioning the British and small 'u' unionist identity into which I was born.
>
> I think the evolution to an Irish identity for me is epitomised by how different the reactions of members of my family to the election of Bobby Sands in the 1981 Westminster by-election were to mine. We were at the funeral of a family member when the news of the election count came through. One family member was literally very angry that Bobby Sands won the contest, whereas I felt that I could understand why. Blood sacrifice, British categorisation by British laws, the nature of the state itself and a British PM with no sense of all of these were factors that I appreciated at the time.
>
> I felt that I could also understand why, within that part of the

Nationalist community which didn't support the armed campaign, those same factors transcended the various attitudes to the IRA and the 'offence' that Bobby Sands was inside for.

Many Unionists were angry. Many of the voices I heard during those days thought that all Nationalists and Republicans had voted for murder. Sands epitomised the IRA. He was part of an illegal organisation who had committed criminal acts and should do his time as a criminal. Giving political status would be a sell-out. They expected many 'hardline' Republicans to vote for him but for the 'softer' Nationalists, they too had voted for murder. Now their true colours were being shown: there was no difference. The fact that the SDLP didn't field a candidate merely showed that when the chips were down, they were all the same.

The election of Bobby Sands was a victory for 'them' [Republicans] with so many actors in the drama, called voters, adding to the confused resentment. This was not just a prisoner in a cell who they read about in a paper or heard about on the TV and radio news. This was a 'criminal', aided and abetted by over 30,000 ordinary people, some of whom were neighbours, teachers and business people – beating the British and Unionists at what the British liked to think was their democracy.

This, to many of them [Unionists], was bringing the worst of the dreadful Troubles for which 'they' [Republicans and Nationalists] were responsible out from the prison where he deserved to be, and allowing him, and Republicans in general, to deliver a victory in an arena they shouldn't even be allowed in. In their view, the election victory had criminalized a community: the community in question had, on the other hand, registered a mass protest against criminalisation. They were poles apart and, as an 'outsider', I was appreciating the mass protest version of events.

I actually remember the anger, frustration and angst at Sands's election more than at his death. At least when he died some of these same people could sneer at his departure; some could even spawn and spread those dark jokes this part of the world is famous for and, most especially of all, Thatcher hadn't given in. She and they lost when Sands was elected but she and they won when he died and some sense of 'justice' was regained.

What these people didn't realise was that it was a pyrrhic victory. I can remember thinking some of that at the time: I am not reading history backwards. When Bobby Sands died, I remember thinking that it was massive, it was going to get worse and there was going to be a real battle for minds. To think of it as victory was a mistake, a tragic mistake.

I can also remember thinking that, as more hunger strikers died, there was a real gap opening up between my own attitudes and those held by many from the Protestant/Unionist community. Their trust in Thatcher grew in tandem with the simplicities of attitudes and thought about the implications. ... they held both this admiration yet distrust that the same lady could ultimately do a deal.

But for me, yes, pressures grew from the [hunger strikers'] families. Fr Faul spoke out, but whether there was going to be six deaths or more it was obvious to me that prison wouldn't be the same again and we were witnessing a major, but obviously tragic, episode. Even by the standards of the Troubles, this was entering psyches in a much more profound way.

However, I cannot say that I saw the deep politicisation ahead, perhaps because I didn't or couldn't really appreciate the network that grew with the many committees around the region. But the now well-known story unfolded and victories, north and south, occurred and anchored quite a profound politicisation of a community.

Chapter Fifteen:

Anglo-Irish agreement

In the aftermath of the hunger strikes, Sinn Fein stunned Loyalists and moderate Unionists alike when Gerry Adams – vice-president of Sinn Fein and, at that time, allegedly a member of the IRA Army Council – was elected to Westminster in 1983 as MP for West Belfast. Up until then, for many years, West Belfast had been a safe seat for the "moderate" SDLP. Adams's election was a deeply disturbing development for Unionists and the British: it appeared that the Nationalist vote in West Belfast was prepared to tolerate IRA violence. And it was a precedent. For many, it showed that the support two years on from Sands's historic victory was not on the wane; if anything, Sinn Fein had converted that support into a deliverable vote of some significance.

The SDLP and the Southern Irish government had good reason to try to stop the rise of Sinn Fein. The SDLP, led by John Hume, had been increasingly critical of the hunger strikes as they went on. This was one factor that lost them votes in West Belfast and other Nationalist areas. The Nationalist electorate, so went the SDLP analysis, was disappointed with "moderate" Nationalism as it had not delivered any progress on the constitutional issue, any improvement in their everyday conditions, any reduction of British soldiers on the ground, or any real evidence of progress on the issue of social justice. Nor did there appear to be any *constructive* dialogue between the SDLP and the Unionists, or with the British. There was certainly dialogue with the British, but it was not really achieving anything. The SDLP impressed upon all who'd listen that, if constitutional Nationalism was ignored by the British government, the government would be forced to deal with Sinn Fein, or at least hand Sinn Fein election victories – one after the other – to the point where "extremist" Republicans eclipsed the SDLP.

The Irish government, on the other hand, certainly was listening to the SDLP. The ruling Fine Gael administration was markedly less well disposed to northern Republicanism than Fianna Fail, to say the least – although northern Republicans would claim neither were any practical help to them. The last thing the Fine Gael leader, Taoiseach Garret Fitzgerald wanted, was for Sinn Fein to become the dominant force in northern Nationalism. The SDLP had always been given a sympathetic hearing in the south of Ireland. Most southern parties shared the SDLP objective of a united Ireland by peaceful means, and with the agreement of the Unionists. While some in Fine Gael might have been happy to forget about the north altogether, others knew that Sinn Fein were on the rise electorally – and had to be stopped.

The southern establishment had been deeply troubled by the election of two H-block prisoners, Kieran Doherty (one of the hunger strikers) and Paddy Agnew, in the Republic of Ireland general election of June 1981. In fact, so close was the result, which eventually saw Fitzgerald form a Fine Gael-Labour coalition, that had the H-block campaign put forward candidates capable of taking their seats in the Dail, they may well have held the balance of power and therefore exercised profound influence on the formation of a government. These members would then have had disproportionate influence on the policy of that government and, bearing mind the context of the time, when the hunger strikes were at their peak, the outcome may have been very different. Some commentators view this as a missed opportunity for Republicans.

Although, it could be claimed that non-prisoner candidates may not have inspired the same level of emotional support. That notion would appear to be contradicted by non-prisoner Owen Carron winning the by-election in Fermanagh-South Tyrone during the hunger strikes in August 1981. However, that constituency had various unique factors going for it. It had been a Republican seat before even Sands had stood for parliament; the previous incumbent, Frank Maguire, being an independent Republican. In addition, the fact that the seat had been won in April by Sands, who, as far as Nationalists were concerned had been allowed to perish by Thatcher's government, made it likely that Nationalist voters would do everything possible to avoid the seat falling to into the hands of Ulster Unionist candidate Ken Maginnes. Fermanagh-South Tyrone had become very much a "Six Counties" seat, so it could reasonably be claimed that the Nationalist electorate in Northern Ireland was politicised to a larger degree than that in the south, especially after the death of several H-block prisoners.

The H-block prisoners' winning of two Dail seats and one Westminster seat was interpreted by the British and Irish establishments as a significant growth in support for, if not all aspects of Republicanism, then at least for the hunger strikes. If allowed to continue, the danger as far as these establishments were concerned was that Sinn Fein would become a significant player in the political development of Northern Ireland. Worse still, from that perspective, the IRA could claim to have broadened its support base and therefore feel encouraged in its violent struggle with the British security forces. It was clear that a strengthened IRA and a reborn Sinn Fein would present war on two fronts, the military and political.

It was also clear that many young Nationalists who had not yet voted could become electoral lobby fodder for Sinn Fein. There was a realisation in some circles that nobody really knew where the ceiling for Sinn Fein's support was, when one took account of such factors as disillusioned potential voters who'd never considered casting a ballot at all being inspired to use their electoral muscle. Sinn Fein and the H-block activists had displayed tremendous organisational skills in getting their vote out. Something had definitely stirred in the Nationalist consciousness. So how would established constitutional Nationalism withstand this new force?

Hume and Fitzgerald were agreed that one answer was to ensure the SDLP were seen to be making real progress on the Nationalist agenda in Northern Ireland. It has to be said, moreover, that the two sincerely wanted progress on the constitutional front and an end to violence. There had to be some new initiative constitutionally because, far from being forgotten by Nationalists, as some among the Unionists and British claimed, the rise of Sinn Fein to more than forty-four per cent of the Nationalist vote from pretty much a standing start showed that Nationalists considered changing the existing constitutional situation to be an issue. Sinn Fein also contested local elections after the hunger strikes and saw their representation grow to more than fifty councillors. Some of this vote was the dormant Republican vote; dormant because Republicans had not contested elections previously, although there had been the odd exception, like McAliskey contesting the European elections on an H-block ticket in 1979. Some Republican votes had been cast for the SDLP in the past but only in the absence of an attractive alternative. So the SDLP would have expected to lose some portion of this reluctant support anyway. But some natural SDLP voters, when presented with the Republican alternative, and in the wake of the hunger strikes, switched. This showed that Sinn Fein could attract SDLP voters. Dublin and London were alarmed.

The Irish government became committed to promoting the interests of the SDLP, as they saw them as the best hope for peaceful progress, in discussions with London. SDLP leader John Hume was a well-respected Westminster MP and carried weight in parliament, particularly with the opposition parties and, to a degree, with the Conservatives whose natural Northern Irish allies were the Ulster Unionist party, led by Jim Molyneaux. Hume's standing helped, but it was the extra pressure exerted at governmental level by Dublin on London that was the real dynamic for a change of approach. This was augmented by the Irish-American lobby in the US, mobilised by sympathy generated during the hunger strikes. This lobby had existed beforehand, and for generations at that, but it was given new impetus by the hunger strikes. US presidents ignored this lobby, one of the most effective in Washington, at their peril. The US did not put pressure on the Thatcher government as such, but made it clear that it would support any initiative that addressed "moderate" Nationalism's concerns. As time went on, the clearer this point was made the more it felt like pressure to the British – albeit of the subtlest nature.

The Thatcher government did not relish the prospect of dealing with Sinn Fein on any level. Supporting the political alternative to Sinn Fein was the natural thing to do, and Thatcher also had to be careful lest she alienate the north's majority Unionist population. But having "faced down" the IRA over the hunger strikes, many Unionists were prepared to invest a degree of faith in her. It should be noted that Unionists traditionally mistrusted all UK governments, believing them to be eager to take the path of least resistance regarding Irish reunification. Thatcher, many believed, was different.

All these elements coming together, some directly, some indirectly as a result of the hunger strikes, meant that it was in the interests of all those seeking to thwart Sinn Fein's political progress to build up the SDLP as a viable alternative. The SDLP were the biggest Nationalist party and for that to remain the case, they needed some results.

Set in this context, the Anglo-Irish agreement of 1985, signed by Thatcher and Fitzgerald's governments, was an indirect result of the hunger strikes. Although other factors played significant roles, too, this was a post hunger-strike attempt to build up support for the SDLP at the expense of Sinn Fein. The agreement was signed four years after the end of the hunger strikes, yet was clearly the culmination of ongoing Anglo-Irish discussions that had opened with talks between Thatcher and the previous Taoiseach, Haughey, in May 1980 (when the H-block protests had been escalating). The dynamic created by that encounter, unquestionably spurred on by the hunger-strike crisis, presaged the New Ireland Forum set up by Fitzgerald. The latter, which ran from May 1983 to May 1984, was attended by the SDLP, Fianna Fail, Fine Gael, and the Irish Labour Party. Unionists had declined to attend, some calling it "nothing but a Nationalist talking shop".

The effect of this "talking shop" was to establish a broad set of principles to which all the constitutional Nationalist parties of Ireland, north and south, could agree. It was this package, albeit distilled by Fitzgerald, that the Irish government would use as a basis for its talks with London. That such talks took place was, again, in part due to the intergovernmental channels opened by Thatcher and Haughey in 1980. A key result of that encounter had been the setting up of an Inter-Governmental Council.

In many ways, these contacts broke some ice that had formed between Britain and Ireland since the failure of the 1973/74 Sunningdale power-sharing agreement. Some found irony in the fact that Thatcher, a British Unionist, and Haughey, leader of the Republican Party as Fianna Fail is also known, could have cordial relations at all – never mind set up contacts that helped pave the way for Fitzgerald's efforts.

These efforts conspicuously excluded northern Republicanism; an irony to some Republicans who have suggested that they would never have happened at all without them. The preliminary discussions took place before the hunger strikes, certainly. But the renewal of high-level official Anglo-Irish contacts in 1980 had in no way guaranteed that those contacts would lead to anything substantial, far less an internationally binding treaty between the two states. And without the Republican hunger strikes of 1981, with the resultant support for Sinn Fein – and the IRA – it is unlikely Thatcher would have agreed to such a wide-ranging deal as the Anglo-Irish Agreement of 1985.

The objective of this agreement was to circumvent the Republican threat by bolstering Hume's SDLP, and the latter were indeed the main beneficiaries. The agreement conceded the SDLP's long-running aspiration for an "Irish dimension" to the governance of Northern Ireland. It formalised, through an inter-governmental secretariat to be based at Maryfield on the outskirts of Belfast, a "consultative role" for the southern government in the running of Northern Ireland. Bearing in mind the Irish government's general concurrence with the SDLP in matters relating to Northern Ireland, many saw this as the Irish government acting in part as a conduit for the SDLP – a conduit with muscle. Unionists believed this gave both the

SDLP, which polled less votes than the Unionists, and the Irish government more of a say in the running of Northern Ireland than they had. Nor were Unionists blind to the possibility that the whole arrangement was a "sop" to the IRA. Although the IRA and Sinn Fein were not the obvious beneficiaries, it was clear the governments had responded to the Nationalist agenda due to pressure brought to bear by Republicans during and in the aftermath of the hunger strikes.

The main four main points of the Anglo-Irish agreement were:

1. The status of Northern Ireland was confirmed as part of the UK, and both governments agreed that this would not change unless the majority of the population in Northern Ireland wanted it to.

2. Both governments agreed to facilitate Northern Ireland rejoining the rest of Ireland if that was what the majority of its inhabitants wished.

3. The Intergovernmental Conference established in 1981 would now consider suggestions from the Irish government regarding the running of Northern Ireland, including security matters.

4. Co-operation on border issues, justice issues and other issues of joint interest.

Some of these points were already in place on a de facto basis, and were a natural evolution of the relationship between two neighbouring states with a common border. What the hunger strikes and the rise of Sinn Fein had clearly done was focus minds on moving at a decent pace and on committing to an agreement. Without the impetus created by the hunger strikes, the determination to sign an agreement that involved substantial compromise and risk is unlikely to have been as strong. That the Conservative and Unionist government of Margaret Thatcher, who had once famously said that Northern Ireland was as British as her own constituency, could concede to the Republic Of Ireland the right to be consulted on Ulster's affairs was a mark of the British resolve to isolate Sinn Fein.

Others, perhaps unsurprisingly, are reluctant to concede that they were mere beneficiaries of a desire to stave off the rise of Sinn Fein during the early 1980s. Sean Farren of the SDLP does not agree that the Anglo-Irish Agreement was solely a response to rising support for Republicans in the wake of the hunger strikes. He also feels that the SDLP were leaders of political change, rather than being swept along by changing political currents, and remains unconvinced that the development of that era precipitated Sinn Fein becoming a legitimate political force. While he concedes that the hunger strikes did have a dramatic impact, to lay too much emphasis on them as an engine of positive change is, he believes, wrong.

> The hunger strikes had overshadowed everything. The tension was palpable. I was chairman of the SDLP at the time. The hunger strikes were not handled properly by the British. It was perhaps the most traumatic event of the Troubles, alongside Bloody Sunday. The hunger strikes gave Sinn Fein a leg-up at a time when the Republican movement desperately needed one. Was it the start of the peace process? I don't think history has "starting points" as such. The hunger strikes encouraged many people to join the IRA, or at least support it in a way they did not previously, as had happened with Bloody Sunday. That influx extended the IRA's campaign by 20 years. It certainly had been flagging before the hunger strikes and the hunger strikes lifted it. But they did also show Republicans a new way forward, too. They helped them find a political voice. Looking back I have sanguine view; the hunger strikes were extremely divisive.

> It [crediting the hunger strikes with the Anglo-Irish Agreement] demeans all other aspects of that agreement. The All-Ireland Forum and then the Anglo-Irish Agreement provide a consensus, a framework for Nationalism. So if others wanted to follow the lead we had shown, so be it. It was not a pan-Nationalist front.

> I acknowledge that the hunger strikers were brave men; brave but wrong. The violence of the IRA was unnecessary. We had democracy, we had the vote, freedom of assembly. There already was a political route for people to follow. And this celebrating of the hunger strikes – there has been a retelling of history in some quarters by some people who have the Republican blinkers on.

> What more could we have done? Well, John Hume was well known in Northern Ireland, but not at that stage was he considered the international statesman he became. He wouldn't have carried enormous weight with Thatcher at that time. Nor would Republicans have held him in high esteem then, either. Regarding now, Sinn Fein have work to do regarding establishing their democratic credentials.

Despite Farren's contention, there are others who suggest that if Sinn Fein had been of a mind to claim credit for the Anglo-Irish Agreement, then they would have had a case to do so. However, Republicans disliked the Agreement as it did not go anywhere near creating a single 32-county Republic Of Ireland. Indeed, this was just another arrangement that "copper-fastened partition" – a view shared by Haughey's Fianna Fail at the time. In fact, Fianna Fail's opposition to the Anglo-Irish Agreement meant that the vote in Dail Eireann to approve it was extremely close: eighty-eight for, seventy-five against.

To give sole responsibility of the Anglo-Irish Agreement to Sinn Fein and the hunger strikes would be to discount the efforts of John Hume over many years, as well as many of those in the Irish and British establishments who worked towards this end. However, many within the Republican movement noted that they had had a significant impact on constitutional events. And if the Unionists were right, that the Anglo-Irish Agreement was a step on the road to a united Ireland, then perhaps a gradualist, political approach had merit. Of course, many military minded Republicans were encouraged in the belief that the armed struggle had pushed the most pro-Unionist British Prime Minister since Churchill into making the concessions contained in the Agreement. If so, then more military action by the IRA was the way forward.

The immediate effect of the Anglo-Irish Agreement was the one intended by the British and Irish governments; namely, that support for Sinn Fein had peaked at around thirteen per cent of the northern Irish vote – forty-four per cent of the Nationalist vote – and was falling back to around ten per cent, or approximately thirty-seven per cent of the Nationalist vote. The Republican electoral bandwagon appeared to have been stopped and, although its core base of ten per cent looked durable, the body-politic of Northern Ireland, Britain and the Irish republic considered that ten per cent to be an acceptable level of political support in that it could be effectively ignored. It was the voters who had gone back to the SDLP that really interested the governments and, with the SDLP vote correspondingly rising, the strategy of empowering the SDLP with tangible political successes such as the agreement was vindicated.

These Nationalist "floating voters", electors who could envisage themselves voting for either Sinn Fein or the SDLP, also greatly interested some strategists in the Sinn Fein camp. They realised that having access to these votes was crucial to growing Sinn Fein taller than "Mr Ten Percent", as the British foreign secretary of the time, Douglas Hurd, disparagingly called Gerry Adams and his party. These voters were impressed with political progress. It could be guessed that they were the Sinn Fein voters least supportive of IRA violence and, indeed, steps were taken within the Republican movement to ensure the IRA exercised "restraint" wherever possible during election campaigns. With that in mind, some in Sinn Fein considered that positive political developments created a mood in which Nationalists might be prepared to vote for Sinn Fein in their greatest numbers. They further considered that anything that could be shown as a step towards the ending of violence would be looked upon positively by the Nationalist electorate.

Such deliberations within Republicanism consolidated the notion of electoral politics playing a part in the "struggle". It is perhaps easy to forget today, when Sinn Fein is the largest Nationalist party in the north and growing in the south, that the very concept of politics being a creditable alternative to armed struggle was by no means accepted by the majority of Republicans. Politics had been "useful", certainly. Those within Republicanism dedicated to developing electoral progress faced the double challenge of keeping their own militant wing on side, while at the same time stemming the significant falling away of electoral support in the wake of the Anglo-Irish Agreement by presenting an image palatable to the Nationalist floating vote.

Some in Sinn Fein claimed that any success the SDLP achieved was due to the impetus provided by Sinn Fein arriving on the political stage, ensuring that the SDLP had to "green itself a bit" in order to appeal to post hunger-strike Nationalist voters. This meant that the SDLP was forced to be stronger in negotiations with the British or anyone else for that matter, so this view continued. Yet if the SDLP had too much success as a result of remaining unchallenged electorally, regardless of the SDLP's underlying motivation, then Sinn Fein ran the risk of allowing the SDLP to became the standard bearers of Nationalism, which, considering what the Republican movement had endured, would be a disturbing development.

Republicans, therefore, needed strategies that did not solely rely on physical force if they were to consolidate their place on the political stage. Some would contend that this is where the current peace process, if conceived by the hunger strikes, came close to being born.

At this time a secret dialogue between Fr Alex Reid – a campaigner for peace and reconciliation who later would be instrumental in the decommissioning process – and Adams had been taking place for a few years. In this dialogue, Reid sought to convince Adams and the IRA of alternative methods to armed struggle. Reid had been a regular visitor to the prisoners in the H-blocks. As this (and other) dialogue developed, Adams became more familiar with the thinking of those out-with the Republican movement and who sought to persuade the IRA to pursue its aims peacefully. This dialogue was not itself a product of the hunger strikes, but it was certainly influenced by them. It arose from an era when Adams and other senior Republicans were considering, if not alternatives to armed struggle, then at least methods additional to armed struggle; and it was continuing in the wake of the Anglo-Irish Agreement and the challenges that presented to Republicans.

Inside the Republican movement, there were those who considered that the Anglo-Irish agreement was an attempt by the British government to "buy off a section of the Nationalist people of the North". Some further considered that as long as Sinn Fein was isolated then partition would be off the political agenda, the rhetoric of the various constitutional Nationalist parties north and south notwithstanding. In the Republic, besides those who were determined to shore up the SDLP as the northern Nationalist vehicle, there were those who gave Republicans the impression that they would gladly forget all about the border as long as they had been "seen to do something". Either way, public alignment with Sinn Fein was not an option for these parties as long as armed struggle was the provisional movement's preferred option.

Opponents of Sinn Fein often suggested, as we have seen, in public utterances that ten per cent of the vote was not significant support. But what some failed to properly consider was that many within that ten per cent went on to become committed and experienced activists and campaigners for Sinn Fein, developing political ideas, electoral plans and strengthening the political infrastructure of the Republican movement. Yes, the vote was tempered by the Anglo-Irish agreement, but the commitment of people at the heart of the Republican movement was not. After the hunger strikes, even when support dipped, it would never go below ten per cent. Some would say that is why the Anglo-Irish Agreement did not finish off Sinn Fein as a political force.

However, Republicans did have to think again on some aspects of their strategy if they wanted to do more than just consolidate that ten per cent. As one source put it, Republicans "took one step back, in order to take two steps forward". The more politicians refused to engage with Sinn Fein, the more some in the Republican movements were convinced that the armed struggle was the only option. Yet others considered that the existence of real political possibilities should be a restraining force on IRA operations to give the movement breathing space to build on such possibilities.

At the Ard Feis of November 1986, Sinn Fein ended the policy of abstentionalism in relation to taking seats in the "partitionist" southern parliament, Dail Eireann. This was seen as a victory for those in Sinn Fein who wanted to develop the political options. Although there was no explicit suggestion of scaling down the armed struggle, far less ending it, the subtext was that ending abstentionalism would have all sorts of implications for the IRA campaign. A minor split in the Provisional movement occurred when the former president of Sinn Fein, Ruairi O'Bradaigh, led small number of his supporters out the conference hall in protest at what they saw as the party's dilution of Republicanism.

The SDLP wanted an end to the IRA campaign. Quite apart from what they saw as its immorality, they saw it as alienating Unionists. They thought Sunningdale, or some version of it, was still an option. However some Republicans thought that if the British ceased to underwrite "every Unionist whim", then they (Unionists) would have to deal with Nationalist and Republicans on a very different level. In the post hunger-strike environment, Republicans would not have settled for Sunningdale revisited. They pointed out that the Unionists would not share power even with the SDLP, or have anything to do with constitutional Nationalism, never mind Republicans. As protests by the Unionist political establishment at the concessions given by the Anglo-Irish Agreement refused to subside, elements of the agreement were watered down in Nationalist and Republican eyes – although fundamentally it remained in place. As long as the British guaranteed "the Unionist veto", an improvement in the underlying situation was not going to change as far as Republicans were concerned. Something, many Republicans thought, had to force the British to think again. In the absence of meaningful Nationalist political pressure, the "cutting edge" of the IRA was the solution for such people.

After Sands and then Carron won the Fermanagh-South Tyrone Westminster seat, the SDLP realised the challenge facing them. The Anglo-Irish Agreement gave the SDLP what many believed was a foundation to consolidate themselves as the main party. Some in that party thought Republicans were the problem, and competitors for the same vote; others thought Republicans could play a part. Indeed, tentative contact had already taken place between the SDLP and Sinn Fein in late 1980 regarding potential ways of co-operating with each other. This had the potential to mirror the tactics of the two main Unionist parties, the Ulster Unionists and the Democratic Unionists, who held the Unionist vote together through an electoral pact that ensured neither stood against each other in Westminster elections. In some constituencies, this joint approach virtually guaranteed a Unionist MP. Over the years, many in the Nationalist community thought their parties should adopt a similar electoral strategy. In 1985, with this in mind, Gerry Adams stated that the possibility of co-operation between the Sinn Fein and the SDLP should be explored.

The upsurge of support for hunger strikers, and subsequently for Sinn Fein, convinced many SDLP activists that their leadership should consider such suggestions positively – although it wasn't until 1988 that the leaderships of both parties formally met. SDLP activists feared losing ground to Sinn Fein. They recognised that Nationalist opinion had been radicalised by the hunger strikes, and sensed the long-term threat posed by Sinn Fein appearing to move in a more constitutional direction. Sinn Fein's public discourse by now included an emphasis on finding solutions to Ireland's divided society. It published *Scenarios for Peace* in 1987. While this document in substance did not suggest a radical departure from Sinn Fein's previous analysis, it at least suggested that Republicans wanted to build on their political base.

Despite some SDLP reservations, the contacts increased gradually after that, allowing the parties to become more familiar with each other's thinking. Both had been at the centre of dramatic moments in recent history; Sinn Fein with the hunger strikes, the SDLP with the Anglo-Irish Agreement. The SDLP implicitly acknowledged the strength and durability of the Republican tradition within wider Nationalism, and Sinn Fein acknowledged that the SDLP carried weight in circles Republicans couldn't get near. There was a sort of mutual respect. Having said that, there were still many Republicans who held the SDLP in contempt – and most SDLP people didn't trust Sinn Fein. Nevertheless, Sinn Fein's evident capacity to harness the electoral support that flowed from the hunger strikes made the party more "respectable" in the north than it had been for sixty years.

The political momentum created by the hunger strikes had clearly driven forward such key developments as the Anglo-Irish Agreement and the cross-party engagement within northern Nationalism. There can be no doubt that a manifest restructuring of the political landscape of Northern Ireland followed in the wake of 1981. Where that restructuring would ultimately end became a vital question in the late 1980s and early 1990s, as Republicans began a campaign to persuade the people of the Six Counties/Northern Ireland, and the wider world, that their ultimate goal was to see all sides lay down their weapons for good and embrace a peaceful political future.

Conclusion

On July 28, 2005, the IRA issued a statement on DVD that read: "All IRA units have been ordered to dump arms." It continued: "All volunteers have been instructed to assist the development of purely political and democratic programmes through exclusively peaceful means." The ballot box was now in both hands.

The statement was read out by Seanna Walsh, a volunteer who had been an H-block OC during the hunger strikes of 1981. Like Walsh, many others in the upper echelons of the present Provisional Republican movement are also veterans of the hunger strikes. Bik McFarlane, former OC of the prison in 1981, still works with the movement as does former hunger-striker Laurence McKeown.

The spirit of the hunger strikes still guides the Provisional movement, though it is impossible to say what the ten men who died would have made of the Good Friday Agreement of 1998 and subsequent peace process. Like their surviving comrades it is most likely that some would have agreed with it, some would have been against it and some would have been somewhere in between. Indeed, the Agreement has not been without its critics from the hunger-strike era. Brendan (the Dark) Hughes, who was leader of the first hunger strike of 1980, is one highly respected opponent of the movement's current direction. A number of former activists point out that nothing will satisfy some Unionists whom, they say, made more fuss about silent IRA weapons than they did about Loyalist weaponry being fired since the IRA cessations. To such former activists, Sinn Fein is walking into a trap.

Nevertheless, after more than a decade of discussion since the IRA cease-fire of 1994 paved the way for the Good Friday Agreement, many Republicans see the dramatic growth of Sinn Fein, to the point where it is now the largest Nationalist party in the north of Ireland, as representing real progress. The silence of Provisional IRA weapons has been a vote-winner. It is nevertheless also a development that owes its origins to the election victories secured by the hunger strikes of 1981.

The electoral success of Sands and his comrades made it possible for Republicans to gradually come to the position that they could one day further their aims via the exclusive pursuit of peaceful politics. As one contributor to this book has vividly illustrated, the hunger strikes consolidated the "old front" of armed resistance for another decade – with new volunteers, money, arms and a level of global support – but they also opened up a "new front" that became the main front over time. The hunger strikes gave Republicans a loud political voice, and the memory of those who died acts like a conscience on the movement. If we accept the religious significance accorded to the events of 1981 by Republican communities, attested to by the many shrines and memorials remembering hunger strikers across the north of Ireland, we can appreciate why the election victories of Sands and others felt like the opening of a "new testament".

Through their dignity, determination and political mandate, the hunger strikers defeated the British campaign of criminalisation, rightly or wrongly. Not only were the prisoners' demands for better conditions widely accepted as just, but the men making them rose in the estimation of Nationalist Ireland – precisely the opposite of what criminalisation was supposed to achieve. If the purpose of the criminalisation policy was to isolate the Republican "men of violence", it was an unmitigated failure.

Some IRA actions continued to appal the public – including their own supporters – with the killing of innocent civilians (Enniskillen for example). However, British government attempts to manufacture a moral distinction between "criminal terrorists" and the perceived state terrorism they called "law and order" were invalidated in the minds of many Nationalists by the conscious self-sacrifice of IRA and INLA volunteers on hunger strike. They were aided in this perception with the growing realisation in the late 1980s and early 1990s that "collusion" was not just a Republican hobby horse, but actually a matter for anyone interested in the rule of law. In post-hunger-strike Ireland, Republican allegations reached a more receptive Nationalist population. And whatever may have been thought of particular operations, the private admission among the British security services that "criminals do not starve themselves to death" resonated for the remainder of the Troubles.

Although the decision to end the 1981 hunger strike allowed the British government to publicly claim they had not "given in to terrorists", this apparent victory was entirely rhetorical. Behind the scenes, the substance of the five demands was quickly conceded. Moreover, the strength and depth of civilian support for the hunger strikers made the British government realise they were facing an enemy that could not be defeated.

This awakened sense of reality prompted the Anglo-Irish Agreement of 1985, the substance of which amounted to a tacit admission that the Nationalist population in the north of Ireland had more sympathy for the IRA than they had for the British government. The election victory of Gerry Adams in West Belfast in June 1983, by demonstrating a clear continuation of the political momentum created by the hunger strikes, left the British in no doubt that radical action was needed to reduce support for what was regarded as the political wing of militant Republicanism. Hoping to divert the constituency awakened by the hunger strikes away from Sinn Fein and towards the SDLP, the British and Irish governments engineered the Anglo-Irish Agreement to demonstrate that the SDLP's more "moderate" way of pursuing the Nationalist agenda could achieve results.

By that time, however, Sinn Fein already had not only an MP but a highly motivated activist base and more than fifty elected councillors. In the view of those Nationalists for whom the Anglo-Irish Agreement was not enough, and impatient for a meaningful improvement in their day-to-day circumstances, Sinn Fein was the party that had that "cutting edge". Attempts to exclude or marginalise Sinn Fein in the 1980s did not acknowledge that its tough political upbringing had given it an infrastructure that was in some ways immune to demoralisation. Thanks to the hunger strikes, the Republican support base was now bigger and stronger than at any time since the Troubles began.

This reawakening of the Republican constituency forced a recognition among the British and the Unionists that the Republican agenda would at some stage have to be engaged, and in a way not seen since partition. As if to challenge repeated British and Unionists assertions that they would accord the Republican perspective proper respect only if they pursued their objectives peacefully, the statement of 28 July on dumping arms was made.

Many hoped a new beginning had arrived. Certainly the British and Irish governments signalled their desire to build quickly upon the development. A further advance, just as dramatic, occurred on Monday September 24, 2005. The IRA decommissioned its weapons in a move verified by General John De Chastelain, chair of the Independent International Commission on Decommissioning in Northern Ireland, and witnessed by two churchmen, one Catholic (Fr Alex Reid) and one Protestant (Rev Harold Good).

Both the British and Irish governments declared themselves impressed.

Unionists, however, remained sceptical. Most notably, the DUP refused to form a government with Sinn Féin. Some Republicans have commented that the continuing percieved intransigence among Unionists demonstrates that the demonising of Republicanism over the last forty years actually has had little to do with a moral abhorrence of the "men of violence". Instead, it is predicated upon Unionism's abhorrence of Republicanism per se, regardless of how peacefully it is pursued. Leading DUP figures continue to express hostility at the prospect of north-south bodies being set up in keeping with the Good Friday Agreement and indeed consider it irresponsible of Nationalists to even mention them. It remains clear that arguing the broad Nationalist position peacefully, calmly and reasonably is deeply unsettling to some Unionists. In the post-hunger-strike world, where the Provisional Republican movement now represents the majority of Nationalists, Unionists don't have to agree with Sinn Féin, but, rightly or wrongly, they do have to listen to Sinn Féin. As the hunger strikes demonstrated, invalidating the whole notion of Republicanism, one of the most durable traditions of the island of Ireland (along with Unionism) is not an option.

Postscript

A sustained assault of Sinn Fein's support base appeared to Republicans to have been launched in the spring of 2005, just ahead of the Westminster elections. This "blitzkrieg of propaganda" brought wave after wave of attack, attempting to highlight IRA brutality, illegal activity and to bring into question the integrity of the Sinn Fein leadership, citing questions over the handling of the hunger strike.

When members of the IRA were said to have been involved in the killing of Robert McCartney in the Short Strand area of Belfast after a pub brawl in February 2005, it provoked a backlash against the IRA and Sinn Fein. A campaign led by McCartney's sisters and fiancée to discover who was responsible for the killing was widely publicised and received support from Unionist politicians, among others. Meanwhile, ongoing killings of Catholics by Loyalist paramilitaries received scant attention, as far as Nationalists were concerned.

The McCartney killing added to controversy arising from the contention of the Irish and British governments that the IRA was involved in the biggest bank robbery in British and Irish history, the Northern Bank robbery of December 2004, in which more than £26 million was stolen from the Northern Bank in central Belfast.

The IRA denied involvement in the Northern Bank robbery and insisted that the McCartney killing involved individuals who, although Republicans at the time, had brought the movement into disrepute and were ejected. Gerry Adams passed names of Sinn Fein members alleged to have been present during the circumstances surrounding the killing to the independent police ombudsman. For many, these high-profile events suggested an unwelcome return to the debate that the hunger strikers had sacrificed so much to win: that the Republican movement is not criminal, but political.

While these controversies inflicted short-term damage on the electoral standing of Sinn Fein, another damaging row erupted that called into question the integrity of the present Republican leadership at a more fundamental level. The power of the hunger strikes to pertain to crucial affairs even a quarter of a century on was illustrated in February 2005. Also illustrated was the willingness of the enemies of Republicanism to use whatever they could to hit back at Sinn Fein. And hitting them on the hunger strikes was hitting at the Republican heart.

This controversy concerned the 1981 hunger strikes and the question of whether or not the leaders of the IRA and Sinn Fein, in order to gain political advantage by prolonging the strikes, withheld from the prisoners an acceptable offer that had been made by the British in July of that year; an offer that would have brought the hunger strikes to a close before McDonnell and the others who followed him died. Figures at the centre of events in July 1981, such as McFarlane and McKeown, categorically reject the assertion, made by Richard O'Rawe in his book *Blanketmen* that the IRA leadership acted duplicitously. McKeown states:

> I think Richard has frozen a moment in time. The hunger strikes were a very fluid situation. For instance, there were hints of offers going on all the time. But nothing was in writing. If it was good enough to offer, it was good enough to put in writing. But of course it never was …
>
> Unless it is in writing, it's not an offer. Why excite people with something that wasn't there? The timing of that book [Blanketmen] was conspicuous, coming before an election and with all the other stuff being flung at Sinn Fein at the time. And it was serialised in the Sunday Times. Now what has the Sunday Times ever done for Republicanism?

Bik McFarlane, whose alleged discussions with O'Rawe form the basis of much of O'Rawe's account, rejects key words and actions attributed to him – without consultation – by O'Rawe. McFarlane considers his former comrade's recollection of events to be fragmentary and confused. McFarlane adds:

> Don't you think that if the Brits had this knowledge, made an offer that had been knocked back by the IRA, that we'd have known about it, either at the time, or at the end of the strikes? Don't you think we'd all know about it by now? Don't you think that they'd have had plenty

of opportunities over the past 20, 25 years to reveal these "great offers" that the IRA supposedly rejected?

We were desperate for a solution. Any deal that went some way to meeting the five demands would have been taken. If it was confirmed in writing, we'd have grabbed it … There was never a deal, there was never a "take it or leave" option at all.

While few interviewed during the research for this book considered O'Rawe or his publishers to have acted with malice or with the deliberate intention of undermining the Republican movement, the timing of the O'Rawe book's publication struck many Republicans as unfortunate. Unfortunate because it appeared to have been seized upon by hostile elements in the British media and political establishments as a propaganda device which, when combined with the furore surrounding the Northern Bank robbery and McCartney killing, made an effective weapon with which to combat the political rise of Sinn Fein and undermine the validity of IRA decommissioning.

With the "war" ostensibly over, there is little doubt that many in the security establishments in both Britain and the Irish Republic have been horrified at Sinn Fein's political progress and the momentum of the IRA's decommissioning exercises. It is now a distinct possibility that Sinn Fein could become a partner in coalition in both the north and the Republic of Ireland, creating a powerful momentum for a united Ireland. To the establishments of both Britain and the Republic, this would threaten major economic and social upheaval.

There are those in British intelligence circles who believe that controversial events of the past year may have been deliberately manipulated in order to trigger a "backlash" to stem the political rise of Sinn Fein. One source for this book, who has been close to intelligence thinking, made the following observation:

You know, if I had been staring at a possible Sinn Fein/DUP coalition in Northern Ireland and a Sinn Fein/Fianna Fail coalition in the Republic, and if I wanted to do everything in my power to stop these things happening, I would have thought it sensible to come up with a plan. Now, some will cry "conspiracy", but maybe that's what plans are.

I'd have feared that the next step was a Gerry Adams bid for presidency and if events went his way, you know, like decommissioning was proven to be done, criminality either hidden well or ceased altogether, then what would have stopped him? Or if not him, then some acceptable face of the Provisionals. If Sinn Fein was in government north and south with a member as President of Ireland, that would create an enormous amount of momentum for a united Ireland. It would perhaps be perceived as an inevitability. That would be destabilizing – and the Unionists wouldn't stand for it.

Now, I would not be surprised if a group of like-minded people got together and said: "Wouldn't it be a good outcome if these things didn't come to pass?" And if it was considered desirable to stop these things happening, then the next step would be: "Right then, what actual means should be employed?" And one that would always occur would be to destroy your foe's credibility within his own natural constituency. This clearly is designed to de-legitimise that person and his cause. Yes, you could say, criminalize and yes, as in the hunger strikes, or more specifically the ending of Special Category Status.

People don't mind rogues – but they hate thugs. It's hard to invent instances, not impossible, but hard. It's much easier to wait, if you have time, until an event or a series of events occur that could be construed to support your analysis. That would signal to the world at large that your opponent's standing in his own community had evaporated and furthermore, it would plant seeds of doubt with his natural supporters. It would also demoralise those actively promoting him and his cause.

I'm not talking of Adams or anyone else here. I'm giving you a hypothetical scenario, one I consider to be not un-typical. In the case of PIRA, it was only a matter of time, I believe, before one or some of their number carried out an act that would inspire revulsion. In other words, perhaps you could say that if it wasn't the McCartney Case, it would have been something else. I say that without wishing to detract for one minute from the horror of that murder.

You must also remember that if there was a campaign against Sinn Fein, and I don't know that there was, then it could have been a defensive measure. The Northern Bank robbery was unprecedented and could finance many things that society doesn't like. I don't believe PIRA intended to go back to war at all. And I'm not convinced it wasn't a "homer" of sorts. However, it still left a lot of financial muscle in dangerous and unpredictable hands.

The prospect of a united Ireland is no longer unthinkable, and there can be no doubt that the political journey that started a quarter of a century ago with the hunger strikes has reached a new and perhaps even more critical stage. In the post-active IRA, the post-decommissioning era, it remains to be seen whether peaceful Republicanism has the capacity to withstand the latest round of propaganda battles. For instance, now that the weapons have been decommissioned, many Unionists have espoused the phrase that republicans need to "decommission their minds", which some interpret as meaning that Republicans must have a political lobotomy before such Unionists will form a government with them. Perhaps more fundamentally, given the history of embedded prejudices outlined in this book, the question remains whether Unionists can accept the large percentage of people in Northern Ireland opposed to partition and discrimination as their political and moral equals. Unionists feel that Republicans have a lot to prove to them, too. They, too, are interested in seeing where the spirit of the hunger strikes leads.

Appendix

The Hunger Strikers

Bobby Sands, MP (27)
Irish Republican Army (IRA) and Member of Parliament (MP)
May 5, 1981, after 66 days.

Francis Hughes (25)
Irish Republican Army (IRA)
May 12, 1981, after 59 days.

Raymond McCreesh (24)
Irish Republican Army (IRA)
May 21, 1981, after 61 days.

Patsy O'Hara (23)
Irish National Liberation Army (INLA)
May 21, 1981, after 61 days.

Joe McDonnell (30)
Irish Republican Army (IRA)
July 8, 1981, after 61 days

Martin Hurson (29)
Irish Republican Army (IRA)
July 13, 1981, after 46 days

Kevin Lynch (25)
Irish National Liberation Army (INLA)
August 1, 1981, after 71 days.

Kieran Doherty, TD (25)
August 2, 1981, after 73 days.

Thomas McElwee (23)
Irish Republican Army (IRA)
August 8, 1981, after 62.

Michael Devine (27)
Irish National Liberation Army (INLA)
August 20, 1981, after 60 days.

The Five Demands:

1. The right not to wear a prison uniform;
2. The right not to do prison work;
3. The right of free association with other prisoners;
4. The right to normal visits, parcels, educational and recreational facilities;
5. Restoration of Remission